A MOMENT WITH ABBA

A 90-day Devotional Journal with Daily
Encouragement, Prayer, & Reflection

BY
DIMITRI THOMAS

Table of Contents

Introduction

We are living in unprecedented and uncertain times that threaten to shake our faith, leave us tired, unmotivated, and ready to give up. In times like these, we need a solid foundation and a growing relationship with Christ to help us cope with life's seismic shocks.

This interactive devotional journal is a great kick start to building a closer relationship with God. Through daily devotion, prayer, and reflection, you can boost your faith, find purpose in Christ, operate in your full potential, and be empowered daily to keep going in life, not give up! The objective is to encourage, empower, and energize those who need it the most through edification and exhortation straight from God and His Word.

This compilation of "Mid-Week Encouragements" done in 2017 was previously sent by me every Wednesday to close friends, family, and social media followers. I did this over the span of 2 years while enduring, eventually fully conquering, and being delivered from a hard season of depression.

Each daily devotional contains empowering words and prayers, as well as an additional writing section for any extra prayer points you'd like to write down. The reflection segment found after each day gives you the opportunity to journal what stood out to you in the devotional, and what you heard God say while reading. You can also use this to jot down how you plan to apply what you read to your daily life or anything else you choose.

As you read this book, may God bless and remind you of His love and plans for you that are so great you will not quit and die prematurely! I pray as you devote 10-20 minutes to God each day through daily devotion, prayer, and reflection that He meets you right where you are with what you need. I stand in agreement with the healing, deliverance, self-forgiveness, promotion, restoration, or anything else you are believing God for. By the end of these 90 days, I speak and claim it done!

Day One

Have you ever felt as if the weight of the world was on your shoulders? You can't stay afloat and everything you do just doesn't work. Do you want to give up? You are not alone. Many have traveled that journey. But in your difficult times, remember God will never put more on you than you can bear. He is sovereign!

God will use the times you feel weakest to manifest His strength in your life. So don't allow the Enemy to con you into isolating yourself, so he can torment and consume you with loneliness. The Enemy will try to change your perspective on what God has said about your situation. Right now, your suffering may seem great but the reward will be greater. Don't give up!

"No test or temptation that comes your way is beyond the course of what others have had to face. All you need to remember is that God will never let you down; he'll never let you be pushed past your limit; he'll always be there to help you come through it" (1 Corinthians 10:13, MSG).

Prayer

Father,

Strengthen me when I feel weak. Let Your strength manifest through my weakness. I know You are sovereign. I experience adversity so You can strengthen my faith and pull out the things You've placed inside of me. I pray against any demon of deception and temptation that may make me come out of agreement of what You promised me while in my temporary season of suffering. I know You do all things well, so I will suffer as You suffered, knowing after I have suffered for a little while, You will call me into Your eternal glory and restore, confirm, strengthen, and establish me.

Amen!

Additional Prayer Points

_____
_____
_____
_____
_____
_____
_____
_____
_____
_____
_____
_____

Reflection

While reading, what stood out to you? What are some things you heard or felt God was saying? What are your key takeaways & how do you plan to apply them to your daily life, or in the future?

_____
_____
_____
_____
_____
_____
_____
_____
_____
_____
_____
_____
_____
_____
_____
_____
_____
_____
_____
_____
_____
_____
_____
_____
_____
_____
_____

Day Two

At times in our lives, God puts us into uncomfortable, difficult, and confusing situations to mature us in Him. Sometimes in that season of growth and maturity, you may fall but that doesn't mean you've failed yourself or God. When you fall, don't stay down. That is when the Enemy will try to attack your mind and make you feel as if you are a failure. He will try to make you believe you can't recover. But don't accept that. When you fall, get right back up. You are already forgiven. There is more to achieve and learn. Even though you've fallen, Jesus still deems you faultless!

"And not only this, but [with joy] let us exult in our sufferings and rejoice in our hardships, knowing that hardship (distress, pressure, trouble) produces patient endurance; and endurance, proven character (spiritual maturity); and proven character, hope and confident assurance [of eternal salvation]. Such hope [in God's promises] never disappoints us, because God's love has been abundantly poured out within our hearts through the Holy Spirit who was given to us" (Romans 5:3-5, AMP).

Prayer

Father,

I thank You for the seasons and situations You use to grow and mature me in You. Help me to adapt. As I do so, help me not to fall into temptation. But if I do fall to past or new temptations, strengthen me to turn away from them, get back up and obey Your will. I pray against any demon of condemnation that will try to keep me complacent if I fall and turn me away from what God has for me. Thank You for loving me enough that when I fall, You present me faultless.

Amen!

Additional Prayer Points

_____

_____

_____

_____

_____

_____

_____

_____

_____

_____

_____

_____

_____

Reflection

While reading, what stood out to you? What are some things you heard or felt God was saying? What are your key takeaways & how do you plan to apply them to your daily life, or in the future?

_____

_____

_____

_____

_____

_____

_____

_____

_____

_____

_____

_____

_____

_____

_____

_____

_____

_____

_____

_____

_____

_____

_____

_____

_____

_____

_____

_____

Day Three

God didn't let you die due to the mistakes you made and the sins you committed in life because Jesus justified you with the blood He shed on the cross. Therefore, don't point out other people's weeds in their gardens when you have some in yours. They too were justified by Christ! In this season, make sure you are learning how to spread the peace, acceptance, love, and positivity of Christ, no matter what the circumstances are. The world needs more people to carry and extend the heart of God.

"Therefore, since we have been justified [that is, acquitted of sin, declared blameless before God] by faith, [let us grasp the fact that] we have peace with God [and the joy of reconciliation with Him] through our Lord Jesus Christ (the Messiah, the Anointed)" (Romans 5:1, AMP).

Prayer

Father,

Thank You for the blood that was shed on Calvary! Thank You for sparing my life all the times I was out of Your will and my mistakes could have killed me! Help me to be a light in this dark world. Help me not to judge but to intercede. Thank You for justifying me in my mess. Help me to continue spreading Your peace, acceptance, love, and positivity to everyone I come into contact with.

Amen!

Additional Prayer Points

_____

_____

_____

_____

_____

_____

_____

_____

_____

_____

_____

_____

_____

Reflection

While reading, what stood out to you? What are some things you heard or felt God was saying? What are your key takeaways & how do you plan to apply them to your daily life, or in the future?

_____

_____

_____

_____

_____

_____

_____

_____

_____

_____

_____

_____

_____

_____

_____

_____

_____

_____

_____

_____

_____

_____

_____

_____

_____

_____

_____

_____

Day Four

You may wonder why God allows you to go through seasons when you can't keep your head above water, and you feel like throwing in the towel. God always uses those times to strengthen your faith in Him. He wants to prove to you that if He brought you through your previous trials, He can surely do it again. He also uses those times to bring out qualities you didn't know you had. These qualities help you to endure difficult seasons and prove to yourself you are stronger than you really are. Remember, whatever you are going through in this season is necessary for the people and places God is sending you to. Therefore, don't give up! Keep the faith and endure because He's already given you the strength to do so.

"Consider it pure joy, my brothers and sisters, whenever you face trials of many kinds, because you know that the testing of your faith produces perseverance. Let perseverance finish its work so that you may be mature and complete, not lacking anything" (James 1:2-4, NIV).

Prayer

Father,

Thank You for every season and trial You've put me through and those I have yet to experience. Thank You that every time I wanted to quit and even when I did throw in the towel, You threw it back at me and told me I have more fight left! Thank You for testing my faith to mature me and for giving me the perseverance to get through the test! I pray against any demon of torment that will try to get me to give up mid-test and miss what You are trying to do in and through me. Thank You that after the test, I won't leave empty-handed. I will gain a new level of maturity and lack nothing.

Amen!

Additional Prayer Points

_____

_____

_____

_____

_____

_____

_____

_____

_____

_____

_____

Reflection

While reading, what stood out to you? What are some things you heard or felt God was saying? What are your key takeaways & how do you plan to apply them to your daily life, or in the future?

_____

_____

_____

_____

_____

_____

_____

_____

_____

_____

_____

_____

_____

_____

_____

_____

_____

_____

_____

_____

_____

_____

_____

_____

_____

Day Five

In life, God allows you to gain and lose friends. Sometimes, He will ask you to give up the favorite possessions you have given priority over Him before He permits certain blessings. Remember, before there is elevation in the spirit, there must be elimination of the flesh. You must remove the distractions and idols that are hindering your relationship with God and stopping you from receiving certain blessings from Him. So the next time your friend walks away or becomes distant, understand that God eliminates certain distractions or takes your idolized possessions away. Don't complain and fight Him because He always blesses those who make sacrifices for His name's sake!

"Whoever finds their life will lose it, and whoever loses their life for my sake will find it" (Matthew 10:39, NIV).

Prayer

Father,

Thank You for every time You eliminated things and people from my life who hindered Your promotions and blessings. I pray that as You continue to circumcise/cut my flesh, separate, and sanctify me, You will give me peace knowing You are sovereign and doing this for Your name's sake. I pray against any rebellious demon that will make me rebel against the new thing You want to do in my life. I pray against those demons that will try to get me to return to the things and people You delivered and separated me from.

Amen!

Additional Prayer Points

_____

_____

_____

_____

_____

_____

_____

_____

_____

_____

_____

Reflection

While reading, what stood out to you? What are some things you heard or felt God was saying? What are your key takeaways & how do you plan to apply them to your daily life, or in the future?

_____

_____

_____

_____

_____

_____

_____

_____

_____

_____

_____

_____

_____

_____

_____

_____

_____

_____

_____

_____

_____

_____

_____

_____

_____

_____

_____

_____

Day Six

The words you speak over your life have power! In fact, they can produce life or death (Proverbs 18:21). God has many words and promises in the Bible that can speak to what you're facing. He has also given you the authority to speak over any situation and circumstance you find yourself in. Therefore, when you speak God's words over your situation, don't continue to worry about it, but go in faith knowing He will work it out in your favor!

> _"God is not a man, that He should lie, nor a son of man, that He should repent. Has He said, and will He not do it? Or has He spoken and will He not make it good and fulfill it?" (Numbers 23:19, AMP)._

Prayer

Father,

Thank You for the Word of God, the Bible. Thank You that everything in it is true, and You've given me the authority to speak what is written in it to my situations, and they change. Help me understand my words have power, and I must not say things out of frustration or tiredness in a certain season. Teach me what to say and how to say it knowing my tongue can produce life and death. I pray against any demon of deception that will try to tell me You are a liar when certain things don't manifest in my time. Let me understand Your timing is always right, and my current season is not a lifetime sentence.

Amen!

Additional Prayer Points

_____
_____
_____
_____
_____
_____
_____
_____
_____
_____
_____
_____

Reflection

While reading, what stood out to you? What are some things you heard or felt God was saying? What are your key takeaways & how do you plan to apply them to your daily life, or in the future?

_____

_____

_____

_____

_____

_____

_____

_____

_____

_____

_____

_____

_____

_____

_____

_____

_____

_____

_____

_____

_____

_____

_____

_____

_____

_____

_____

_____

Day Seven

When God elevates and moves you to different areas in life, you will experience growing and transition pains, but that's life. When He exposes you to new standards and outlooks, sometimes it's so out of the norm, you want to give up and go back to the last level you were on, but don't quit! Things may feel different right now but keep your faith and trust God to mold, shape and adapt you into the person He wants you to be in your new season.

"In You, O Lord, I have placed my trust and taken refuge; Let me never be ashamed; In Your righteousness rescue me. But as for me, I trust [confidently] in You and Your greatness, O Lord; I said, "You are my God" (Psalm 31:1, 14, AMP).

Prayer

Father,

Thank You for elevating and promoting me even when I didn't want to be. Thank You for being with me and holding my hand when I experience growing pains from the elevation and transition to new seasons. As I continue to adapt in my new seasons, help me not to get weary and complacent in the process. Instead, give me the endurance I need to finish the race You've set before me to achieve the prize of the high calling. I pray against any demon of complacency that will try to keep my mindset complacent because the process wasn't what I thought it would be.

Amen!

Additional Prayer Points

_____

_____

_____

_____

_____

_____

_____

_____

_____

_____

_____

Reflection

While reading, what stood out to you? What are some things you heard or felt God was saying? What are your key takeaways & how do you plan to apply them to your daily life, or in the future?

_____
_____
_____
_____
_____
_____
_____
_____
_____
_____
_____
_____
_____
_____
_____
_____
_____
_____
_____
_____
_____
_____
_____
_____
_____
_____
_____

Day Eight

There are times in life you will feel as if you can't reach the next level. You believe your visions won't ever manifest and opportunities will never find you. Hence, you get comfortable and complacent. God has called you to do more; therefore, you can't afford to become lackadaisical. God has given you all the necessary tools to be the best you can, achieve every goal, and reach the next level in life.

Whenever God gives you opportunities and visions, you must move and act in faith. Trust God's plan that everything will work out, but in His timing. Remember God will never give you a vision without the access to provision.

> **"Let us not grow weary or become discouraged in doing good, for at the proper time we will reap, if we do not give in" (Galatians 6:9, AMP).**

Prayer

Father,

Thank You for giving me the endurance I need, so I won't be complacent and want to give up on seeing the visions and new levels in life through. Continue to give me the tools I need to achieve every goal I set for myself and reach new levels in You. Strengthen my faith when I find myself in a season of waiting, knowing that waiting produces patience and hope. In due season, I will reap a harvest.

Amen!

Additional Prayer Points

_____

_____

_____

_____

_____

_____

_____

_____

_____

_____

_____

_____

Reflection

While reading, what stood out to you? What are some things you heard or felt God was saying? What are your key takeaways & how do you plan to apply them to your daily life, or in the future?

_____
_____
_____
_____
_____
_____
_____
_____
_____
_____
_____
_____
_____
_____
_____
_____
_____
_____
_____
_____
_____
_____
_____
_____
_____
_____

Day Nine

We have all done things in life we aren't proud of, but don't let the thought of your past rob you of what God has for you in the present. God gives us grace and mercy that is renewed every morning. He teaches us He forgives us, but we should forgive ourselves as well. Therefore, if you keep living your life based on your past, you won't be able to move forward to the things of God and walk in your true identity. The Enemy is making you hold yourself a hostage of your past. He does this to stop you from walking in the things of God. Remember, there is a reason why the windshield is bigger than your rearview mirror.

> *"If we say that we have no sin, we deceive ourselves, and the truth is not in us. If we confess our sins, He is faithful and just to forgive us our sins and to cleanse us from all unrighteousness. If we say that we have not sinned, we make Him a liar, and His word is not in us" (I John 1:8-10, NKJV).*

Prayer

Father,

Thank You for Your grace and mercy that I receive every new day! Help me to forgive myself for my sins as You have forgiven me. Take away all guilt and shame that will try to hold me in bondage and keep me from doing the things You have called and commissioned me to do. Thank You that my future is much bigger than my past, which is a steppingstone to get me to where I need to be: the good, bad, and ugly. Help me not the dwell on the past but use it as a testimony in the present.

Amen!

Additional Prayer Points

_____

_____

_____

_____

_____

_____

_____

_____

_____

_____

_____

Reflection

While reading, what stood out to you? What are some things you heard or felt God was saying? What are your key takeaways & how do you plan to apply them to your daily life, or in the future?

_____
_____
_____
_____
_____
_____
_____
_____
_____
_____
_____
_____
_____
_____
_____
_____
_____
_____
_____
_____
_____
_____
_____
_____
_____
_____
_____

Day Ten

You may not be where you want to be right now in life. Whether spiritually, academically, physically, or otherwise, the goal in life isn't to do better than the next person. Rather, it is to do better and strive to be better every chance you get. So, don't beat yourself down for not reaching certain goals or completing certain tasks. God doesn't reward you based on the goals you set for yourself, but your faith, diligence, and perseverance while completing them. Stop going through life setting goals, mapping ideas, and writing visions down, then quitting the moment adversity comes. Learning to accept adversity when it comes will help you fight through it to get to the blessing that's on the other side!

"And not only this, but [with joy] let us exult in our sufferings and rejoice in our hardships, knowing that hardship (distress, pressure, trouble) produces patient endurance; and endurance, proven character (spiritual maturity); and proven character, hope and confident assurance [of eternal salvation]. Such hope [in God's promises] never disappoints us, because God's love has been abundantly poured out within our hearts through the Holy Spirit who was given to us" (Romans 5:3-5, AMP).

Prayer

Father,

Thank You for every season of adversity I've had to face, because it pushed me to where I am today. Thank You for the authority You have given me over adversity. Help me to change my negative mindset when I am trying to reach goals and complete tasks in life. You faced adversity but didn't let it overtake You. I pray against any demon of comparison that will try to make me compare myself to others when I see them completing goals, as well as receiving promotions and blessings, because I know mine are on the way!

Amen!

Additional Prayer Points

_____

_____

_____

_____

_____

_____

_____

_____

_____

_____

_____

Reflection

While reading, what stood out to you? What are some things you heard or felt God was saying? What are your key takeaways & how do you plan to apply them to your daily life, or in the future?

_____

_____

_____

_____

_____

_____

_____

_____

_____

_____

_____

_____

_____

_____

_____

_____

_____

_____

_____

_____

_____

_____

_____

_____

_____

_____

_____

Day Eleven

This year, month, week, or even day may not have been the best for you thus far. It may have left you tired, stressed, or disappointed but the fact you've made it this far means God still has a plan and purpose for your life. You have gone through many things to get to where you are right now; although you might not be where you want to be, give God praise that you aren't where you used to be. The Enemy sees you're tired, so he will try to manipulate and deceive you to give up, but don't give up, push through! God sees your tears and labor. He sees your sleepless nights. Keep pushing! Keep striving! Keep working! God didn't bring you this far to leave you.

"Let us not grow weary or become discouraged in doing good, for at the proper time we will reap, if we do not give in" (Galatians 6:9, AMP).

Prayer

Father,

Thank You for every day You have seen me through. Thank You for the plan and purpose You have on my life. Help me to live it out until You call me to be with You. I pray against every demon that will try to manipulate and deceive me to turn against God and what He has said to and about me.

Amen!

Additional Prayer Points

_____

_____

_____

_____

_____

_____

_____

_____

_____

_____

_____

_____

_____

_____

_____

Reflection

While reading, what stood out to you? What are some things you heard or felt God was saying? What are your key takeaways & how do you plan to apply them to your daily life, or in the future?

_____

_____

_____

_____

_____

_____

_____

_____

_____

_____

_____

_____

_____

_____

_____

_____

_____

_____

_____

_____

_____

_____

_____

_____

_____

_____

_____

_____

_____

_____

Day Twelve

The hardest thing in life is to trust God when it seems as though things in your life aren't going right. But as hard as it sounds, God has a specific plan and purpose for everything that happens in your life: good or bad. Just because things aren't going the way you planned doesn't mean God didn't plan them to go that way and that it won't work out for your good. God can change any situation you find yourself in, but you must simply trust Him and His plan. It's very easy to give up on your plans when things go wrong. And that's what the Enemy wants you to do. Therefore, pray and ask God to increase your faith where it's weak and your endurance if it seems low, so when trials come your way, you can keep going. God can and He will work it out in your favor.

"And we know that all things work together for good to those who love God, to those who are the called according to His purpose" (Romans 8:28, NKJV).

Prayer

Father,

Thank You for the plan and purpose You have for my life. I am grateful that since I love You, and I'm called according to Your purpose that everything I go through in life will work out for my good. Thank You for giving me endurance and strength to go through all that is in Your plan for me: good and bad. Help me to understand everything I go through is to strengthen me, my faith, and my mindset. I pray against every demon that will come and try to knock me off course and make me quit when things don't go the way I planned.

Amen!

Additional Prayer Points

_____

_____

_____

_____

_____

_____

_____

_____

_____

_____

_____

Reflection

While reading, what stood out to you? What are some things you heard or felt God was saying? What are your key takeaways & how do you plan to apply them to your daily life, or in the future?

_____

_____

_____

_____

_____

_____

_____

_____

_____

_____

_____

_____

_____

_____

_____

_____

_____

_____

_____

_____

_____

_____

_____

_____

_____

Day Thirteen

Many times, we get so bogged down with our responsibilities that we prioritize them above God. You may feel as though you have so much going on that you can't catch a break. Everything is happening all at once, and you are trying to keep a smile on your face. However, when you feel burdened with the trials of life, seek God, and enter His presence. Seek God daily because only He can bring peace, comfort, and joy in your life. The more you seek Him and His presence, the more peace and joy you will have.

"You will keep in perfect and constant peace the one whose mind is steadfast [that is, committed and focused on You—in both inclination and character], Because he trusts and takes refuge in You [with hope and confident expectation]. Trust [confidently] in the Lord forever [He is your fortress, your shield, your banner], For the Lord God is an everlasting Rock [the Rock of Ages]" (Isaiah 26:3-4, AMP).

Prayer

Father,

Thank You for the peace, comfort, and strength I receive in Your presence. Thank You that I can come boldly before Your throne of grace and obtain mercy and freedom from everything that is bogging me down. Keep me in Your perfect peace as long as I seek You daily! Forgive me for every time I prioritized and exalted my problems over You. I pray against every demon that will try to come and take my peace and strength when I am burdened.

Amen!

Additional Prayer Points

_____

_____

_____

_____

_____

_____

_____

_____

_____

_____

_____

_____

_____

_____

Reflection

While reading, what stood out to you? What are some things you heard or felt God was saying? What are your key takeaways & how do you plan to apply them to your daily life, or in the future?

_____

_____

_____

_____

_____

_____

_____

_____

_____

_____

_____

_____

_____

_____

_____

_____

_____

_____

_____

_____

_____

_____

_____

_____

Day Fourteen

In life, you may go through storms that make you question God's love for you. You wonder if He cares or if He loves you why He would make you go through such difficult times. While in your storm, the Enemy will try to attack your mind. He will make you feel alone and abandoned. He will also try to turn you away from God based on your present situation. God permits certain storms in your life to strengthen your faith. He is sovereign and knows how much you can bear. Also, He takes you through certain storms to show Himself mighty. That way, when He delivers you, He is the only one who gets the glory. As you go on in life, you may find yourself in a season of depression, discouragement, bereavement, low self-esteem, etc. In spite of this, don't question God's love for you. Don't get upset at His silence in a season or let the Enemy deceive you. Remain in prayer. Stay faithful to God and His Word and He will bring you through! Remember, the teacher never talks during a test.

"When the righteous cry [for help], the Lord hears and rescues them from all their distress and troubles. The Lord is near to the heartbroken And He saves those who are crushed in spirit (contrite in heart, truly sorry for their sin). Many hardships and perplexing circumstances confront the righteous, but the Lord rescues him from them all" (Psalm 34:17-19, AMP).

Prayer

Father,

Thank You for every storm You have permitted in my life and delivered me from. You did so to strengthen my faith and show Yourself mighty on my behalf. I pray that whenever a storm is permitted in my life, that I will hold onto Your track record. You have delivered me out of many other storms, and You've never left me. I pray against any demon that'll make me quit in the storm because I know on the other side is a blessing and a promotion.

Amen!

Additional Prayer Points

_____

_____

_____

_____

_____

_____

_____

_____

_____

_____

_____

_____

_____

Reflection

While reading, what stood out to you? What are some things you heard or felt God was saying? What are your key takeaways & how do you plan to apply them to your daily life, or in the future?

_____

_____

_____

_____

_____

_____

_____

_____

_____

_____

_____

_____

_____

_____

_____

_____

_____

_____

_____

_____

_____

_____

_____

_____

_____

_____

_____

_____

Day Fifteen

In life, you will experience much hurt, pain, trials, and tribulations. In some instances, your experiences will cause wounds that will take some time to heal. Although you may not see it now, God is using the pain from your wound to strengthen and lead you to your purpose in life. After you've been healed, you will also have a scar that will tell the story of your wound. It will testify of the hurt and pain you overcame while healing. Therefore, don't cover up or be ashamed of your scars. The stories you share about how you endured and overcame, may help someone else to endure the pain and/or healing they may be going through.

> *"Oh, thank God —he's so good! His love never runs out. All of you set free by God, tell the world! Tell how he freed you from oppression, Then rounded you up from all over the place, from the four winds, from the seven seas. Oh, thank God —he's so good! His love never runs out. All of you set free by God, tell the world! Tell how he freed you from oppression, Then rounded you up from all over the place, from the four winds, from the seven seas. Oh, thank God —he's so good! His love never runs out. All of you set free by God, tell the world! Tell how he freed you from oppression, Then rounded you up from all over the place, from the four winds, from the seven seas" (Psalm 107:1-3, MSG).*

Prayer

Father,

Thank You for every scar I have, as well as each wound I had to endure. Thank You for delivering me. Thank You that every scar I have tell a story of what I have been through. Help me not to be ashamed of the things I had to go through to get to where I am today. I pray against any demon that will put a muzzle over my mouth or shame me so I won't tell others the testimony of my scars.

Amen!

Additional Prayer Points

_____

_____

_____

_____

_____

_____

_____

_____

_____

_____

_____

_____

Reflection

While reading, what stood out to you? What are some things you heard or felt God was saying? What are your key takeaways & how do you plan to apply them to your daily life, or in the future?

_____

_____

_____

_____

_____

_____

_____

_____

_____

_____

_____

_____

_____

_____

_____

_____

_____

_____

_____

_____

_____

_____

_____

_____

_____

_____

_____

Day Sixteen

In life, it's easy to plan your future, goals, and where you want to be by a certain time. However, you will eventually get to a point in your life where you feel stuck. You don't know what move to make or where to even begin. The Enemy will make you feel abandoned, alone, and as if God hasn't heard your prayer for guidance. However, it's in those times, where God is not only able to show you what steps you should take, but also manifest His plan and purpose for your life and what path He wants you to take. You have to understand that God isn't worried about what your will is. He's worried about His will being manifested in your life for His glory. Therefore, don't let the Enemy deceive you into thinking your plan is better than God's. God's plan is to make you prosper. He does not want to harm you. However, if you follow your plan, you will fall into harm's way and not prosper.

"Trust in and rely confidently on the Lord with all your heart and do not rely on your own insight or understanding. Do not be wise in your own eyes; Fear the Lord [with reverent awe and obedience] and turn [entirely] away from evil. In all your ways know and acknowledge and recognize Him, And He will make your paths straight and smooth [removing obstacles that block your way]. It will be health to your body [your marrow, your nerves, your sinews, your muscles—all your inner parts] and refreshment (physical well-being) to your bones" (Proverbs 3:5-8, AMP).

Prayer

Father,

Thank You for helping me through my time in the wilderness when I felt as if no one was around, and I was stuck in my current season unable to get a prayer through. Thank You, Lord, for always hearing and guiding me through the wilderness to get to the promised land. Give me an ear to listen to Your voice, not those around me or the Enemy's. Help me to trust Your plan for my life and not my plan because Your will shall be done. I pray against any demon that will make me want to give up in my wilderness season while being burnt out or discouraged thinking God has forgotten me.

Amen!

Additional Prayer Points

_____

_____

_____

_____

_____

_____

_____

_____

_____

_____

_____

_____

Reflection

While reading, what stood out to you? What are some things you heard or felt God was saying? What are your key takeaways & how do you plan to apply them to your daily life, or in the future?

_____

_____

_____

_____

_____

_____

_____

_____

_____

_____

_____

_____

_____

_____

_____

_____

_____

_____

_____

_____

_____

_____

_____

_____

_____

Day Seventeen

You may find yourself burdened down, but it's not because of the trials you are facing in your life. Rather, it's because you are rushing your will. You are not fully submitting to God's will or waiting on His plans and purpose to manifest in your life in His timing. When you desire and do things in your timing, you tend to grow tired, stressed, burnt out, and lost. However, if you truly take the time to process and seek God to see why He has you in a certain season, you will find peace and hope in your now. You will not be discouraged about getting to your next point outside of the timing of God. Wait on God and in due season, you *shall* reap if you faint *not*!

> *"But those who wait for the Lord [who expect, look for, and hope in Him] shall change and renew their strength and power; they shall lift their wings and mount up [close to God] as eagles [mount up to the sun]; they shall run and not be weary, they shall walk and not faint or become tired ([Hebrews 12:1-3] Isaiah 40:31, AMPC).*

Prayer

Father,

Thank You for giving me the patience to wait on Your will and time. Thank You for not allowing me to receive anything before Your time for me to have it. You are sovereign and all-knowing. Help me to understand You make us wait for certain things to teach us lessons in our now. I pray against the Enemy of distraction that will try to block the big picture during my waiting season. I also pray against any demon that will try to come and make me tired and want to give up.

Amen!

Additional Prayer Points

_____

_____

_____

_____

_____

_____

_____

_____

_____

_____

Reflection

While reading, what stood out to you? What are some things you heard or felt God was saying? What are your key takeaways & how do you plan to apply them to your daily life, or in the future?

_____

_____

_____

_____

_____

_____

_____

_____

_____

_____

_____

_____

_____

_____

_____

_____

_____

_____

_____

_____

_____

_____

_____

_____

_____

_____

_____

Day Eighteen

The Enemy entices you with many worldly things to deter and distract you from doing what God has called you to do. His intention is to prevent you from fulfilling your purpose and visions, reaching your destiny, or simply living like Christ. When you entertain or participate in worldly lifestyles, it will steer you off the path God specifically designed to help you reach your destiny in His timing; that's what the Enemy wants. Pray and ask God daily to allow the Holy Spirit to strengthen you, so you may live like Him. Ask God to help you resist distractions and the temptations of the world but also to get rid of any old mindsets and habits that are holding you hostage from reaching your destiny.

> *"Finally, be strong in the Lord and in the strength of his might. Put on the whole armor of God that you may be able to stand against the schemes of the devil. For we do not wrestle against flesh and blood, but against the rulers, against the authorities, against the cosmic powers over this present darkness, against the spiritual forces of evil in the heavenly places. Therefore take up the whole armor of God, that you may be able to withstand in the evil day, and having done all, to stand firm" (Ephesians 6:10-13, ESV).*

Prayer

Father,

Forgive me for every time I give in to worldly distractions and partake in things I know will knock me off the path You have set for me. God, help me turn away from evil, so it will flee from me. Continue to rid me of the things and people I don't need in my life that will delay my destiny. I pray against any demon of distraction that comes when I am on course to where God wants me to go. I pray against deception when I am tired, depleted, and ready to give up on the plan and call of God. Thank You for strengthening me when I want to give in to temptation. Continue to help me turn away when it comes.

Amen!

Additional Prayer Points

_____

_____

_____

_____

_____

_____

_____

_____

_____

_____

_____

Reflection

While reading, what stood out to you? What are some things you heard or felt God was saying? What are your key takeaways & how do you plan to apply them to your daily life, or in the future?

_____
_____
_____
_____
_____
_____
_____
_____
_____
_____
_____
_____
_____
_____
_____
_____
_____
_____
_____
_____
_____
_____
_____
_____
_____
_____
_____
_____

Day Nineteen

Many times, we get so busy and stressed out in life that the Enemy makes us feel weary, depleted, stuck, and hopeless. At these times, we make decisions based on our fear(s), instead of our faith. The Enemy loves to manipulate the minds of those who are tired and weary. However, God will use difficult situations to show us our weaknesses. When we realize we are weak, we have no choice but to pray to Him. God has granted us the ability to go to Him in prayer and obtain His guidance, love, strength, mercy, and grace. Therefore, whenever the Enemy makes you dwell in your weaknesses, pray and ask God to manifest His strength. In the end, He is bigger than our problems, worries, and stress. Don't magnify your problems over God. Instead, magnify God over your problems, so He can demagnify your problems and increase your faith.

"Therefore let us [with privilege] approach the throne of grace [that is, the throne of God's gracious favor] with confidence and without fear, so that we may receive mercy [for our failures] and find [His amazing] grace to help in time of need [an appropriate blessing, coming just at the right moment" (Hebrews 4:16, AMP).

Prayer

Father,

Thank You for bringing me through every time I felt so weak and depleted I wanted to give up. Thank You for guiding and giving me strength in my weakest times of life. I pray that when I feel weak, I won't make decisions based on my feelings in the moment but on my faith and what You have already said. I pray against any spirit that will cause me to prematurely abort anything God has designed for me to go through. I know it was done to make my relationship with Him, my faith, and me stronger.

Amen!

Additional Prayer Points

_____

_____

_____

_____

_____

_____

_____

_____

_____

_____

_____

_____

Reflection

While reading, what stood out to you? What are some things you heard or felt God was saying? What are your key takeaways & how do you plan to apply them to your daily life, or in the future?

_____

_____

_____

_____

_____

_____

_____

_____

_____

_____

_____

_____

_____

_____

_____

_____

_____

_____

_____

_____

_____

_____

_____

_____

_____

_____

_____

Day Twenty

You may be at a point in your life where you become stuck and stagnant in your faith. In your season of stagnation, the Enemy will try to distract you from your purpose because he knows your potential and influence in and for the body of Christ. The Enemy will always try to diminish your hope and destroy your faith! When he destroys your faith, you have fallen into the pit of his schemes, under his power, and the rulers of darkness. Therefore, do not let the Enemy manipulate your mind. Don't let him convince you to give up your faith in God, deter you from doing what God has called you to do or consistently say yes to God in any season you find yourself. Remember, the greater the Enemy's attacks, the greater and closer you are to your breakthrough. So don't give in to his distractions, schemes, and tactics!

> *"So let God work his will in you. Yell a loud no to the Devil and watch him scamper. Say a quiet yes to God and he'll be there in no time. Quit dabbling in sin. Purify your inner life. Quit playing the field. Hit bottom, and cry your eyes out. The fun and games are over. Get serious, really serious. Get down on your knees before the Master; it's the only way you'll get on your feet"* (James 4:7-10, MSG).

Prayer

Father,

Thank You for giving me the authority over the Enemy, so whenever he comes to distract and deter me, I can tell him to flee, and he has no choice but to do so. Thank You that even when I am stagnant and stuck in my faith, You are still faithful to me. Help me not to be stuck in my faith. Move me from glory to glory in every aspect of my life, including my faith, anointing, and purpose. I pray against any spirit of deception that will try to knock me off the course You set, make me lose my hope and faith in God, and bring me under subjection to the rulers of darkness.

Amen!

Additional Prayer Points

_____

_____

_____

_____

_____

_____

_____

_____

_____

_____

_____

Reflection

While reading, what stood out to you? What are some things you heard or felt God was saying? What are your key takeaways & how do you plan to apply them to your daily life, or in the future?

_____

_____

_____

_____

_____

_____

_____

_____

_____

_____

_____

_____

_____

_____

_____

_____

_____

_____

_____

_____

_____

_____

_____

_____

_____

_____

_____

_____

Day Twenty-One

You will experience storms in your life. It's inevitable. The Enemy will make you feel as if God purposely put you in a place where He isn't present or listening. The Enemy will make you feel every attack, storm, and temptation is purposely meant for your downfall. He will make you feel lonely, isolated, and neglected, but that is a lie! The Bible tells us Jesus was made like us. He was sent to the world in the flesh just like us, "His brethren." He went through the same sufferings, trials, and tribulations we face here on the earth today. This made Him merciful, faithful, and able to relate to us. Therefore, the next time you feel helpless, hopeless, or alone in a storm, call on the name of Jesus and seek Him. He is 100% man and 100% Divinity (God), so He can and will help you. He will see you through whatever you find yourself in because He truly knows your pain and how you feel.

"Therefore, it was essential that He had to be made like His brothers (mankind) in every respect, so that He might [by experience] become a merciful and faithful High Priest in things related to God, to make atonement (propitiation) for the people's sins [thereby wiping away the sin, satisfying divine justice, and providing a way of reconciliation between God and mankind]. Because He Himself [in His humanity] has suffered in being tempted, He is able to help and provide immediate assistance to those who are being tempted and exposed to suffering" (Hebrews 2:17-18, AMP).

Prayer

Father,

Thank You for sending Your Son to the earth in the flesh to take on the same sufferings, trials, and tribulations I go through. Jesus, I thank You for being merciful to me and interceding on my behalf that even when I fall into sin, bondage, and temptation, You still deem me faultless, and love me unconditionally. I pray that when the Enemy tries to come and make me feel lonely, isolated, and neglected when the storms come that I draw closer to You, and You draw closer to me, so I can hear what You have to say. I pray against any spirit that will try to make me dwell in isolation, abandonment, and fall into a dark place. Surround me with people I can trust, those who hear from You and pray for me when my faith is too low to pray for myself.

Amen!

Additional Prayer Points

_____

_____

_____

_____

_____

_____

_____

_____

_____

_____

Reflection

While reading, what stood out to you? What are some things you heard or felt God was saying? What are your key takeaways & how do you plan to apply them to your daily life, or in the future?

_____
_____
_____
_____
_____
_____
_____
_____
_____
_____
_____
_____
_____
_____
_____
_____
_____
_____
_____
_____
_____
_____
_____
_____
_____
_____
_____
_____

Day Twenty-Two

The Enemy loves to use the hardships of loss and trials to make you lose faith, quit the call of God, stop what you've been working toward, and turn against God. When the Enemy sees he can't take you out, he will do anything to weigh you down and make you turn away from God, as well as what He has promised you. But remember if God is for you, then who or what can be against you (Romans 8:31)?! When you are in the storm, it is not the time to stray from God. Rather, you should draw closer to Him and see what He has to say while you are in the storm. Sometimes, God won't eliminate your storms, but He will step in it with you. Everything God permits in your life, whether good or bad, is for a reason and a season. In the end, it will make you and your faith stronger. Therefore, hold on and keep your faith in God. Know it's okay to cry when things get overwhelming and hard because your tears water the seed of your blessing to come. Those who sow tears reap joy in the end.

"And we know [with great confidence] that God [who is deeply concerned about us] causes all things to work together [as a plan] for good for those who love God, to those who are called according to His plan and purpose"(Romans 8:28, AMP).

Prayer

Father,

Thank You for every season of life You permitted me to go through, whether good or bad. I pray that while in my bad seasons and storms, You will help me to hold onto Your promises and be steadfast and immovable. I pray that when I feel like giving up in the storm, You will give me the strength and endurance to continue to walk because eventually, I will walk out of the storm. I pray against any demon that will try to make me give up or turn away from God in my storm because I know God's plan is to prosper me, as long as I am in His will.

Amen!

Additional Prayer Points

_____

_____

_____

_____

_____

_____

_____

_____

_____

_____

_____

_____

_____

Reflection

While reading, what stood out to you? What are some things you heard or felt God was saying? What are your key takeaways & how do you plan to apply them to your daily life, or in the future?

_____
_____
_____
_____
_____
_____
_____
_____
_____
_____
_____
_____
_____
_____
_____
_____
_____
_____
_____
_____
_____
_____
_____
_____
_____
_____
_____
_____

Day Twenty-Three

In your life, you will have many trials and tribulations. The Enemy will try to put a muzzle over your mouth to hinder your praise because he understands if he can hinder your praise, he will hinder your blessings and breakthroughs. Praise is a weapon: *"As they began to sing and praise, the Lord set ambushes against the men of Ammon and Moab and Mount Seir who were invading Judah, and they were defeated"* (2 Chronicles 20:22). You may be in a season of depression, loss, stagnation, lack, etc., right now. However, if you learn to turn the pressures of life into praise, you can stand still, and watch God turn your battle into a breakthrough and blessing. Remember, there is a reason for every season God permits in your life. Your temporary season is *not* a lifetime sentence.

> *"Praise be to the Lord, for he has heard my cry for mercy. The Lord is my strength and my shield; my heart trusts in him, and he helps me. My heart leaps for joy, and with my song I praise him" (Psalm 28:6-7, NIV).*

Prayer

Father,

Thank You for the ability to freely praise Your name! I thank You that I can use praise as a weapon against the Enemy. Whenever the Enemy comes up against me, my praise will make him flee. I pray that when the Enemy tries to muzzle my mouth and intimidate me so I won't praise You openly that You would remind me of the things You've brought me through. I pray against the Enemy who will try to keep me bound, complacent, and silent when I should be worshipping and praising You. Make me a free worshipper in every season I go through.

Additional Prayer Points

_____

_____

_____

_____

_____

_____

_____

_____

_____

_____

_____

_____

_____

Reflection

While reading, what stood out to you? What are some things you heard or felt God was saying? What are your key takeaways & how do you plan to apply them to your daily life, or in the future?

_____
_____
_____
_____
_____
_____
_____
_____
_____
_____
_____
_____
_____
_____
_____
_____
_____
_____
_____
_____
_____
_____
_____
_____
_____
_____
_____

Day Twenty-Four

There will come a time, you will encounter certain situations that will make it seem as if God has left you by yourself, although that is not the case. The Enemy will try to make you feel God has left you high and dry and has gone against His Word. Sometimes, God will use certain situations to test your faith level, response, and prayer life. He does this to see if you will operate in fear or use the authority and power He has given you to pray about and speak to your situations. God has given us the same authority He has through the Holy Spirit. 2 Timothy 1:7 says, *"For God hath not given us the spirit of fear; but of power, and of love, and of a sound mind."* Therefore, the next time you find yourself in a difficult situation, and it seems as if God has forsaken you, remember God has given *you* the spirit of power to speak to a thing and cause it to cease.

Remember, tests happen at the end of a course. Therefore, when you find yourself in a season of testing, you will pass the test and be promoted to a new season and level in glory. But to do so, you must utilize everything God taught you in that season!

> *"I assure you and most solemnly say to you, whoever says to this mountain, 'Be lifted up and thrown into the sea!' and does not doubt in his heart [in God's unlimited power], but believes that what he says is going to take place, it will be done for him [in accordance with God's will]. Jesus replied, "Have faith in God [constantly]"* (Mark 11:22-23, AMP).

Prayer

Father,

Thank You for never leaving me or forsaking me, even when You are quiet for a season, and it feels as though you have left me. Thank You for giving me the power to speak Your Word to my situations to bring about change because Your Word will not return to You void. You stand on Your Word. So even when the Devil tries to make me give up in a testing season, I stand on every word and prophecy You speak. Although they may not manifest in my timing, I know they will come to pass. When I reach the testing season, I am at the end of a thing.

Amen!

Additional Prayer Points

_____
_____
_____
_____
_____
_____
_____
_____
_____
_____
_____
_____
_____

Reflection

While reading, what stood out to you? What are some things you heard or felt God was saying? What are your key takeaways & how do you plan to apply them to your daily life, or in the future?

_____
_____
_____
_____
_____
_____
_____
_____
_____
_____
_____
_____
_____
_____
_____
_____
_____
_____
_____
_____
_____
_____
_____
_____
_____
_____
_____
_____
_____

Day Twenty-Five

The time will come when God will strip you of your fleshly and worldly desires, mindsets, and peers. These are the people and things in your life that will distract you from hearing His voice. They prevent the full anointing from flowing and stop God from blessing you abundantly. God doesn't want to allow things to happen in your life prematurely or without you being in the right posture to receive it. He will strip things from you, which He will use to bless you for His glory. Be careful to give into worldliness, because it will taint the goodness, favor and blessings He wants to manifest in your life. When you feel God stripping and cutting your flesh, don't be reluctant, disobedient, and rebellious against what He is doing or telling you to do.

Let go of the things He is cutting out of your life and learn to walk in the newness He's attempting to create in your life. He simply wants to position you for His greater anointing and blessings. Whenever you feel yourself falling for fleshly desires, pray against them! Remember, full obedience to and sacrifice for God is better than the applause of man and fulfilling the wants of the flesh.

"For what will it profit a man if he gains the whole world [wealth, fame, success], but forfeits his soul? Or what will a man give in exchange for his soul? For the Son of Man is going to come in the glory and majesty of His Father with His angels, and then He will repay each one in accordance with what he has done. For whoever wishes to save his life [in this world] will [eventually] lose it [through death], but whoever loses his life [in this world] for My sake will find it [that is, life with Me for all eternity]" (Matthew 16:25-27, AMP).

Prayer

Father,

Thank you for stripping me of certain things & removing certain people, that would cause me to not clearly hear what you would have to say. I pray that you would help me understand that cutting & pruning is apart of growing & cultivation. I know that you would never remove or separate me from something without reason. So, help me to change my mindset when it happens, because I know everything you do & allow in my life, will work for my good. I thank you that my flesh is coming into subjection to the spirit & that my spirit man is stronger than my flesh. I pray against the enemy that will cause me to be rebellious and try to convince me to not let go or run back to the things, people & places you told me to stay away from.

Amen!

Additional Prayer Points

_____

_____

_____

_____

_____

_____

_____

_____

_____

Reflection

While reading, what stood out to you? What are some things you heard or felt God was saying? What are your key takeaways & how do you plan to apply them to your daily life, or in the future?

_____

_____

_____

_____

_____

_____

_____

_____

_____

_____

_____

_____

_____

_____

_____

_____

_____

_____

_____

_____

_____

_____

_____

_____

_____

_____

_____

Day Twenty-Six

The statement "Objects in mirror are closer than they appear" is engraved on most, if not all side mirrors of today's vehicles. Often times, we go through life dwelling on the past, how it hurt us, broke us, and how we messed up and failed. God is saying He wants to do a new thing, but you keep looking in your side mirror at things of the past. Consequently, the Enemy magnifies the problems to make them look closer than they actually are. The Enemy knows if he can condemn you and keep you bound by your past, you will also be distracted and unable to see the new things God is doing and wants to do in your life. If this happens, you won't walk in the fullness of your future with God. Therefore, don't let the Enemy torment you and use the objects of your past to steer your focus off what God is doing now and wants to do in the future.

> *"Do not remember the former things, or ponder the things of the past. Listen carefully, I am about to do a new thing, now it will spring forth; Will you not be aware of it? I will even put a road in the wilderness, Rivers in the desert"* *(Isaiah 43:18-19, AMP)*

Prayer

Father,

Thank you that I don't have to live in bondage to my past! My past does not define who I am today & although the enemy will try to bring up my past, I know that I have been forgiven and freed from it! I ask that you help me not to dwell on the things that I did & went through in past seasons. Your word declares that we overcome by the blood & the power of our testimony, so help me to not be ashamed of sharing my past experiences if it will help bring deliverance to someone else. I pray that any devil that tries to condemn me for my past be cast out of my mind & that you would fill the void with the Holy Spirit.

Amen!

Additional Prayer Points

_____

_____

_____

_____

_____

_____

_____

_____

_____

Reflection

While reading, what stood out to you? What are some things you heard or felt God was saying? What are your key takeaways & how do you plan to apply them to your daily life, or in the future?

_____
_____
_____
_____
_____
_____
_____
_____
_____
_____
_____
_____
_____
_____
_____
_____
_____
_____
_____
_____
_____
_____
_____
_____
_____
_____
_____

Day Twenty-Seven

You may be in or will eventually enter a season where God is calling you to submit and walk in the thing(s) He has called you to. Or you may find yourself in an area of life where you are still figuring out what that call is; that's okay! Continue to seek God and in due time, He will reveal it to you.

You may have answered the call but you are not operating fully in the call because of denial, intimidation, and fear. Or you may be operating fully in the call but not at the level God desires. Many people know the call of God but have put it on "call waiting." They haven't answered the call. This is disobedience, and rebellion. Yes, you may feel unworthy, fearful, doubtful, and much more, but the Enemy will use those debilitating emotions to keep you complacent, disobedient, and not submitted to God, so you won't answer His call. Remember, Romans 8:30 declares, *"And those he predestined, he also called; those he called, he also justified; those he justified, he also glorified."* God has predestined and justified you specifically for His call! He is simply waiting on your "yes" to Him, so He can give you the next set of instructions! What will your answer be? Your future depends on your "yes," and your yes is not only for you, but it's also about somebody else.

> *"Now yield and submit yourself to Him [agree with God and be conformed to His will] and be at peace; in this way [you will prosper and great] good will come to you"(Job 22:21, AMP).*

Prayer

Father,

Thank You for wanting to use someone like me. Thank You for the calling You have placed on my life. Help me to fulfill the call to the best of my ability until the day You call me home. God, show me how to walk boldly in the calling. You didn't give me a spirit of timidity and fear but of power, love, and a sound mind. So give me a sound mind to believe walking in Your calling will bring me prosperity and provision, and You will help me to operate in love as You love us. I pray against the spirit of complacency, fear, disobedience and rebellion that will try to keep me from operating as You have called me to.

Amen!

Additional Prayer Points

_____

_____

_____

_____

_____

_____

_____

_____

_____

_____

_____

_____

Reflection

While reading, what stood out to you? What are some things you heard or felt God was saying? What are your key takeaways & how do you plan to apply them to your daily life, or in the future?

_____
_____
_____
_____
_____
_____
_____
_____
_____
_____
_____
_____
_____
_____
_____
_____
_____
_____
_____
_____
_____
_____
_____
_____
_____
_____
_____
_____

Day Twenty-Eight

At some point in your life, God will place you in a season of lack, not as a punishment, but as a lesson. He will do this when you have become too self-reliant and consumed with worldly things, instead of solely relying on Him and seeking His righteousness. While in this season, He will teach you to stop depending so much on yourself to make things happen in your life and stop seeking worldliness. He wants you to truly seek Him first! If you find yourself in a season of lack, don't let the Enemy trick you into thinking God has forsaken you because He hasn't. Once you learn to humbly seek Him and His righteousness first without any expectations, He will give you what you need and the desires of your heart, because you would have tapped into His desires for you. Not only that, He will restore the things you lost with better and then some because you endured the season of lack. Therefore, don't quit in your season of lack! In it, there's a lesson and a test. After, you'll reap a harvest and receive a reward!

> *"But first and most importantly seek (aim at, strive after) His kingdom and His righteousness [His way of doing and being right—the attitude and character of God], and all these things will be given to you also" (Matthew 6:33, AMP).*

Prayer

Father,

I thank You for every season You take me through. Some may be hard to endure and in others, I may want to throw in the towel. However, both the good and bad seasons are for a reason. Thank You, Lord, that in a season of lack, You are right there with me. Help me to seek You with a sincere and humble heart, so I may find You and get to know You better. Help me to know You desire more than what I desire for myself and to receive the things You have for me, I must continuously seek You and You only, not the things and people of the world. Thank You that after the season of lack You will restore what was lost with better and more.

Amen!

Additional Prayer Points

_____

_____

_____

_____

_____

_____

_____

_____

_____

_____

_____

Reflection

While reading, what stood out to you? What are some things you heard or felt God was saying? What are your key takeaways & how do you plan to apply them to your daily life, or in the future?

_____

_____

_____

_____

_____

_____

_____

_____

_____

_____

_____

_____

_____

_____

_____

_____

_____

_____

_____

_____

_____

_____

_____

_____

_____

_____

_____

_____

Day Twenty-Nine

You get to a point in your life when you may find yourself in a season of discomfort. It may be in your faith, job, friendship, marriage, or even your relationship with God. He realizes that placing you in a season of discomfort will push you to your potential and destiny in Christ. In this season, the Enemy will try to keep you bound to where you used to be. Most of this happens in your mind. The Enemy will try to condemn you because of your past and deter you from remaining faithful during this season. However, you must mature and operate in what God is calling you to. Know that everything you have gone through this season is a part of God's divine plan. There are gifts, ministries, and a stronger anointing you have yet to tap into, but your comfort has kept you in complacency, and you remain where you are. God wants to release you in this season, but you must be willing to be uncomfortable. Don't allow the Enemy to pull you away from the new thing God wants to do in and through you and the new places, He wants to take you to.

"Do not remember the former things, or ponder the things of the past. Listen carefully, I am about to do a new thing, Now it will spring forth; Will you not be aware of it? I will even put a road in the wilderness, Rivers in the desert" *(Isaiah 43:18-19, AMP).*

"For this reason I remind you to fan into flame the gift of God, which is in you through the laying on of my hands. For the Spirit God gave us does not make us timid, but gives us power, love and self-discipline" *(2 Timothy 1:6-7, NIV).*

Prayer

Father,

Thank You for the new thing You are doing in my life even if I don't see it. I say yes and surrender to Your will and the new thing You want to do. Walk close to me as I go through my seasons of discomfort. I pray against any distractions that may try to knock me off course to make me quit and go back to where I was comfortable. Help me let go of places, people, and mindsets that will bring me back to my comfort zone. Fill me with Your Holy Spirit so when I reach a place where I don't know what to do, He will tell me where to go and what to do.

Amen!

Additional Prayer Points

_____

_____

_____

_____

_____

_____

_____

_____

_____

_____

_____

_____

Reflection

While reading, what stood out to you? What are some things you heard or felt God was saying? What are your key takeaways & how do you plan to apply them to your daily life, or in the future?

_____
_____
_____
_____
_____
_____
_____
_____
_____
_____
_____
_____
_____
_____
_____
_____
_____
_____
_____
_____
_____
_____
_____
_____
_____
_____
_____
_____
_____

Day Thirty

A time will come in your life where you become fully submitted and walk in the things God has called you to do, but you don't submit to the process that comes with the calling. You must go through a specific process to bear fruit, reap a harvest, and receive the powerful anointing God wants to give you. Purpose isn't about the destination but the journey and process of getting there. It is so easy to give up on what God has called you to do and go the other way. After you give Him a complete yes, things get absolutely harder than they were before you said yes. You may be in a season of lack, loss, pain, heartache, depression, confusion, and so forth. Whatever you are in, do not give up on the call or the process!

A promise is at the end of your process. Your yes is not just for you, but it is about the people and places you are called to. God is simply testing your faith to see if it is strong enough to handle His promise. Remember, those who experience great pressure from their process will produce great oil so keep going!

> *"I consider that our present sufferings are not worth comparing with the glory that will be revealed in us. For the creation waits in eager expectation for the children of God to be revealed" (Romans 8:18-19, NIV)*

Prayer

Father,

Thank You for walking with me through the process of my calling. Thank You for never leaving me and for giving me the endurance I needed to get through the hardest part of the process. Continue to uphold and carry me through as I walk in what You have called me to. I pray against the Enemy who will try to come in and manipulate my mind during the tough times. Renew my mind and give me peace in the middle of the hard times. I know that the process won't be easy, but it will be worth going through because on the other side, You have a promise, anointing, and a new level of favor for me.

Additional Prayer Points

_____

_____

_____

_____

_____

_____

_____

_____

_____

_____

_____

_____

_____

Reflection

While reading, what stood out to you? What are some things you heard or felt God was saying? What are your key takeaways & how do you plan to apply them to your daily life, or in the future?

_____

_____

_____

_____

_____

_____

_____

_____

_____

_____

_____

_____

_____

_____

_____

_____

_____

_____

_____

_____

_____

_____

_____

_____

_____

_____

_____

Day Thirty-One

In life, the people, situations, and mindsets you let influence you will hinder you from hearing the voice of the Lord and fully walking in your calling, anointing, and potential. Therefore, God has to let them spiritually die in your life to supernaturally resurrect and give life to new and better people who will strengthen the anointing and call on your life. Yes, it will be hard. You will want to go back to the things you had, but that is what the Enemy wants. He wants to keep you bound to old mindsets, and old ways. That way, he will prevent you from moving closer to what God desires for you and wants to bring out of you. So when you feel the urge to go back to your old ways, know that you are on the right track and the Enemy is trying to turn you away from what God has for you in the end.

> *"Brothers, I do not consider that I have made it my own. But one thing I do: forgetting what lies behind and straining forward to what lies ahead, I press on toward the goal for the prize of the upward call of God in Christ Jesus" (Philippians 3:13-14, ESV).*

Prayer

Father,

Thank You so much for ridding me of the old mindsets, friends, and ways that kept me away from seeking You more and walking fully in my calling and anointing. Thank You for always being gracious and patient, even when I pushed back after You took away things to make me better. I pray against the Enemy who will try to tempt me to go back to the old things. I know when he tempts me with the old You are springing up something new. So help me to continue to press toward the mark even when it gets hard, when I feel alone or led astray. I know You are always with me; You will never leave me.

Amen!

Additional Prayer Points

_____

_____

_____

_____

_____

_____

_____

_____

_____

_____

_____

Reflection

While reading, what stood out to you? What are some things you heard or felt God was saying? What are your key takeaways & how do you plan to apply them to your daily life, or in the future?

_____

_____

_____

_____

_____

_____

_____

_____

_____

_____

_____

_____

_____

_____

_____

_____

_____

_____

_____

_____

_____

_____

_____

_____

_____

_____

Day Thirty-Two

YOU ARE CALLED AND ANOINTED!

Yes, you! The Enemy is so afraid of you walking in your calling that he is trying to throw every obstacle and temptation your way to slow you down, make you turn away from God, and give up on what God has called you to do in this season. God is preparing you to take down the Enemy's kingdom, and he is afraid. He is scared of the powerful things God has birthed inside you. Don't give up! Your test is temporary. The Enemy may look as if he is winning sometimes, but God will turn the bad situations around to work in your favor and prove to the Devil You are stronger than the forces of hell. Therefore, if you ever feel you are ready to give up in the time of adversity, don't! It's usually when you are ready to give up that God is about to elevate you to a new level.

> *"And those whom he predestined he also called, and those whom he called he also justified, and those whom he justified he also glorified. What then shall we say to these things? If God is for us, who can be against us?"(Romans 8:30-31, ESV).*

Prayer

Father,

Thank You for calling me! Whether I know where I am called to, who I am called to, or what I am called to do, thank You for putting me on the earth to fulfill it! Thank You for creating me to resolve a specific problem on the earth. Help and equip me to do what You have called me to do. Show me how to do it for Your glory and not my own. I pray against anyone or anything that stands in my way of walking in the call of God. I pray against the Enemy that will try to make me feel unworthy, fearful, and want to run away from Your call, or try to make me turn away and quit in the process. I know going through the process will produce the person for the call! Thank You for that plan over my life. I will see it manifest!

Amen!

Additional Prayer Points

_____

_____

_____

_____

_____

_____

_____

_____

_____

_____

_____

Reflection

While reading, what stood out to you? What are some things you heard or felt God was saying? What are your key takeaways & how do you plan to apply them to your daily life, or in the future?

_____

_____

_____

_____

_____

_____

_____

_____

_____

_____

_____

_____

_____

_____

_____

_____

_____

_____

_____

_____

_____

_____

_____

_____

_____

_____

Day Thirty-Three

Sometimes, you may find yourself in a crisis and the only person who can turn the situation around is God. In crisis, you must always be in a humble posture of prayer. The Bible tells us to pray without ceasing, but we must also pray without worrying. Prayer is an essential tool of 2-way communication with our heavenly Father. Yes, prayer is a time where we lay our petitions down. God also uses that time to talk back to us; we must be patient and wait for Him to speak. Although this sounds backward, God talks to us the most during chaotic times. The problem is we allow the chaos to distract us and take precedence over the voice of God. Hence, we miss the strategies, words, and confirmation we need during the crisis. In prayer, we gain peace. If we neglect prayer, we abandon the very thing God gives us through the Holy Spirit, which is peace (a fruit of the Spirit). We may not always (if ever) get the very thing we're petitioning for in the moment of prayer, but God always grants us peace until the petition is granted or He tells us otherwise.

> *"Do not be anxious about anything, but in everything by prayer and supplication with thanksgiving let your requests be made known to God. And the peace of God, which surpasses all understanding, will guard your hearts and your minds in Christ Jesus" (Philippians 4:6-7, ESV).*

Prayer

Father,

Thank You for the direct access we have to communicate with You through the Father, which is prayer! Thank You for always giving me peace during chaos even when it feels as if everything around me is going crazy. Thank You for speaking even more during chaotic times. Help me to hear Your voice and not allow the distractions around me to take precedence over Your voice and what You are saying! Thank You for the strategy, wisdom, chastisements, and even affirmation You give me in prayer! I pray against the Enemy who will try to throw me off course and make me stagnant in my prayer life. Help me to stay consistent in Your Word and in prayer. In your Word, I gain the knowledge I need to pray, and through prayer, I can lay my petitions down, hear Your voice, and gain strategies from You to go through life.

Amen!

Additional Prayer Points

_____

_____

_____

_____

_____

_____

_____

_____

_____

Reflection

While reading, what stood out to you? What are some things you heard or felt God was saying? What are your key takeaways & how do you plan to apply them to your daily life, or in the future?

_____

_____

_____

_____

_____

_____

_____

_____

_____

_____

_____

_____

_____

_____

_____

_____

_____

_____

_____

_____

_____

_____

_____

_____

_____

_____

_____

_____

Day Thirty-Four

God has given you so many prophetic words, visions, and dreams. Sometimes, it seems as if He has forgotten about them, but He hasn't. He is more than able to bring them to pass, but He is waiting for the right time to do so. While you're waiting, remain faithful, ready, and in the right posture! While you're waiting, continue to have faith because the Enemy will try to manipulate your mind and make you think God is not going to bring them to pass. The Devil will make you think you're crazy for having these dreams and visions and believing they will manifest, but reject him. When God blesses you with the things He promised you, remain humble and faithful. Use everything for His glory knowing that without Him, nothing would be possible.

"God is not man, that he should lie, or a son of man, that he should change his mind. Has he said, and will he not do it? Or has he spoken, and will he not fulfill it?" (Numbers 23:19, ESV).

Prayer

Father,

Thank You for fulfilling every word, promise, and dream You gave me. I may have had to wait, but waiting produces patience, so thank You for allowing me to wait and be patient for some things I am not ready for or for which I need to mature before getting. Increase my faith in my waiting season and allow me new perspectives while waiting. Thank You for not being a person to lie or repent. Thank You for meaning everything that comes out of Your mouth and that You don't repent for saying them. I thank You that You won't take back the promises, visions, or words you gave. You will not repent for giving them to me. I pray against the Enemy who will try to manipulate my mind to make me think otherwise.

Amen!

Additional Prayer Points

_____

_____

_____

_____

_____

_____

_____

_____

_____

_____

_____

Reflection

While reading, what stood out to you? What are some things you heard or felt God was saying? What are your key takeaways & how do you plan to apply them to your daily life, or in the future?

_____

_____

_____

_____

_____

_____

_____

_____

_____

_____

_____

_____

_____

_____

_____

_____

_____

_____

_____

_____

_____

_____

_____

_____

_____

_____

_____

_____

_____

Day Thirty-Five

Often times, God will put you in places and seasons of discomfort at the very time you become complacent where you are. During the uncomfortable season, you will want to give up and go back to your place of complacency because you feel you aren't getting the breakthrough you thought you would. The Enemy loves to attack when He sees you're in an uncomfortable season. He knows at that time you are more vulnerable and susceptible to give in to his tactics and temptations that will draw you away from God, make you reach your breaking point, give up and go back to your complacent place, wherever, or whatever that may be. If you learn to conquer your breaking point in seasons of uncomfortability, you'll receive a breakthrough! Therefore, when you feel you can't press through uncomfortable situations and seasons in your life, pray, have faith, and conquer them because on the other side is a breakthrough!

"Be strong and courageous. Do not fear or be in dread of them, for it is the Lord your God who goes with you. He will not leave you or forsake you" (Deuteronomy 31:6, ESV).

Prayer

Father,

Thank You for never leaving me when You place me in a season of uncomfortability. Thank You for always leading and guiding me to where You need me to go. Increase my endurance and perseverance as I continue to journey through those seasons. Give me the wisdom I need to operate while trying to find comfortability in uncomfortable seasons. I pray against the Enemy who will try to make me turn away and go back to my place of contentment and complacency. I know You place me in these seasons to grow, mature, and pull out the potential I didn't know I had in me. Therefore, I ask that You help me to find peace in being uncomfortable.

Amen!

Additional Prayer Points

_____

_____

_____

_____

_____

_____

_____

_____

_____

_____

_____

Reflection

While reading, what stood out to you? What are some things you heard or felt God was saying? What are your key takeaways & how do you plan to apply them to your daily life, or in the future?

_____
_____
_____
_____
_____
_____
_____
_____
_____
_____
_____
_____
_____
_____
_____
_____
_____
_____
_____
_____
_____
_____
_____
_____
_____
_____
_____
_____

Day Thirty-Six

Be careful! Don't let the Enemy distract you with different mindsets and memories of your past. Sometimes in your life, he will make you look at things from the wrong perspective. He will also make you focus and dwell on the struggles, loss, pain, and mistakes of your past. He will continue to condemn you to the point where you will miss what God has for you and what He wants you to do in a new season and realm in Him. If He hasn't already, God is ready to reveal the blueprint and visions He has for us, but we are too focused on what was or wasn't, what we don't have, who isn't or wasn't there, etc. Truth be told, God isn't worried about that because He wrote out our journey to begin with. He knew the struggles, hurt, and pain we would have to heal from. However, you cannot continue to let the Enemy use your past to hinder and distract you from what God is doing and about to do!

Ask yourself what the Enemy is holding over your head to distract you from seeing the *new* God is doing in your *now*.

> *"Remember not the former things, nor consider the things of old. Behold, I am doing a new thing; now it springs forth, do you not perceive it? I will make a way in the wilderness and rivers in the desert"* (Isaiah 43:18-19, ESV).

Prayer

Father,

Thank You for everything I've had to go through to get to where I am today: the good, bad, and ugly. Thank You for Your divine plan and purpose for everything I have gone and will go through in life. I thank You for the testimony I already have that will help someone along the way who has been or currently is in my former position. Don't let me be ashamed of my past but help me to be bold and share my testimony with those I need to. May my testimony help them overcome the situation they are facing in their lives. I pray against the Enemy who continues to condemn me for my past. Remind me that I am a new creature because I am in You. Help my identity in Christ become a reality to me.

Amen!

Additional Prayer Points

_____

_____

_____

_____

_____

_____

_____

_____

_____

_____

Reflection

While reading, what stood out to you? What are some things you heard or felt God was saying? What are your key takeaways & how do you plan to apply them to your daily life, or in the future?

_____

_____

_____

_____

_____

_____

_____

_____

_____

_____

_____

_____

_____

_____

_____

_____

_____

_____

_____

_____

_____

_____

_____

_____

_____

_____

_____

_____

_____

Day Thirty-Seven

Stop having survivor's remorse! You survived what may have taken other people out for a reason. God graced you to survive that season, situation, relationship, sickness, or whatever it was, for a reason! God wants to use your story and testimony of survival to help people through or bring others out of what you went through. That's why you're still here! Therefore, no matter what happened, what you experienced to get to where you are today, and what the Enemy threw at you to knock you off course, congratulations! You made it through, and you are still here, which means God has a plan, purpose, and calling on your life for you to fulfill. Don't let the Enemy make you feel as if you shouldn't be here because others didn't survive what could've taken you out. God's grace and mercy kept you through it all and that makes your testimony just that much greater!

> *"O give thanks to the Lord, for He is good; For His compassion and lovingkindness endure forever! Let the redeemed of the Lord say so, whom He has redeemed from the hand of the adversary" (Psalm 107:1-2, ESV).*

Prayer

Father,

Thank You for everything I have been through to get to where I am today! I know everything works together for the good of those who are called according to Your purpose, those who love You. So I thank You that all of the good and bad I went through in my life work for good. I thank You for my testimony. I pray that it will help free others who are experiencing what I went through. Help me not to be ashamed of my testimony and that You help me to be a blessing to others by sharing my experiences with them. I pray against the Enemy who will make me feel bad for surviving things that may have produced other outcomes for different people. I thank You for Your continued grace and favor on my life! I don't take it for granted that I am still here, so since I am, help me to boldly walk in what You have called me to walk in.

Amen!

Additional Prayer Points

_____

_____

_____

_____

_____

_____

_____

_____

_____

Reflection

While reading, what stood out to you? What are some things you heard or felt God was saying? What are your key takeaways & how do you plan to apply them to your daily life, or in the future?

_____

_____

_____

_____

_____

_____

_____

_____

_____

_____

_____

_____

_____

_____

_____

_____

_____

_____

_____

_____

_____

_____

_____

_____

_____

_____

_____

_____

_____

Day Thirty-Eight

It's only a matter of time, if you haven't already, before you will hear the actual voice of God for the first time. You will hear it and understand it's not your thoughts or even the Enemy. When you begin to shut out distractions, seek the Lord and His face, you will begin to hear His voice. When you become intentional about your time with God, He will draw close to you and even tell you to do things you may or may not want to do. However, when you are obedient to Him, there are no limits to the blessings and doors He'll open. It will get very hard at times because the Enemy will fight against you. He will do everything in his power to make you turn around and quit. That way, you won't follow through with what God has told you to do or believe. You will not come into full agreement with the promises of God in your life.

God will surround you with friends, mentors, colleagues, and others who will push you, hold you accountable, pray for you through the good and bad or to simply be a friend and listening ear! When you walk closely with God, hear, and be obedient to His voice and direction, He will bless you so much you will be in awe. That doesn't excuse you from the trials and the lessons of process you have to go through, but it will be well worth it. God will help you catch up to where you are supposed to be in His divine plan because you are obedient to Him.

"Yes indeed, it won't be long now." GOD's Decree. "Things are going to happen so fast your head will swim, one thing fast on the heels of the other. You won't be able to keep up. Everything will be happening at once—and everywhere you look, blessings" (Amos 9:13-15, MSG).

Prayer

Father,

Thank You for the chance to talk to You through prayer but also hear Your voice. I thank You that I don't worship someone who is deaf or dumb, but I worship someone who sees, hears, and talks back. I thank You for every strategy, affirmation, and chastisement You give me when talking to me because it reminds me of Your love for me. As I continue my walk with You, Your voice becomes louder than my distractions, friends, life, and even my own thoughts. I pray against anything that may hinder Your voice from being heard in my life. I pray that as You talk, I listen and obey, no matter how I feel about what You have told me to do.

Amen!

Additional Prayer Points

_____

_____

_____

_____

_____

_____

_____

_____

_____

_____

_____

_____

Reflection

While reading, what stood out to you? What are some things you heard or felt God was saying? What are your key takeaways & how do you plan to apply them to your daily life, or in the future?

_____
_____
_____
_____
_____
_____
_____
_____
_____
_____
_____
_____
_____
_____
_____
_____
_____
_____
_____
_____
_____
_____
_____
_____
_____
_____
_____

Day Thirty-Nine

In life, if you don't learn to sacrifice and give up the thing(s) God recognizes will plague your future, they will definitely plague you! God is sovereign and all-knowing, so He tells you to get rid of things for a reason, especially when He sees they will not benefit you but will be detrimental to the call and purpose on your life. They can come in any form but are usually people in your life whom God may tell you to separate from in a certain season or forever because they could bring you down. They may be hindering you from walking in your full anointing by keeping you bound by your past or even tempting you to do things outside of what God has told you to do. Therefore, when God tells you to separate yourself from certain people, do it without hesitation. It could be the very thing hindering your blessing, deliverance, or even an opportunity from God. If God gives you the opportunity while you are connected to them it could be detrimental. The life God has for you is far better than the life you think is best for you.

> *"He who finds his life will lose it, and he who loses his life for my sake will find it" (Matthew 10:39).*

Prayer

Father,

Reveal those things or people You want me to sacrifice, so I can draw closer to You and what You have for me. Help me to understand You know the plan for me. It's to prosper and not harm me. Therefore, anything You tell me to sacrifice is to prosper me. You will reward me in the long run for doing so. I pray against the Enemy who will make me want to go back to the things You told me to separate from because they will do nothing but continue to plague me and what's inside of me. Give me the endurance to do whatever it takes to press toward the mark of the prize of Your high calling.

Amen!

Additional Prayer Points

_____

_____

_____

_____

_____

_____

_____

_____

_____

_____

_____

Reflection

While reading, what stood out to you? What are some things you heard or felt God was saying? What are your key takeaways & how do you plan to apply them to your daily life, or in the future?

_____
_____
_____
_____
_____
_____
_____
_____
_____
_____
_____
_____
_____
_____
_____
_____
_____
_____
_____
_____
_____
_____
_____
_____
_____
_____
_____
_____

Day Forty

Toxins are poisonous substances that can live in our bodies. Although they may live in our bodies, they are dangerous. If we don't flush them out, they can harm us. Similarly, having toxic people in our circles can be harmful to us. We connect ourselves to toxic people in life because if we are honest, we too were toxic and sometimes can still be toxic.

As we drink more and more water we start to flush those toxins out of our bodies, Likewise, when we consume more of "The Living Water," Jesus, His Word, His love, His acceptance, His affirmation, and His rebuke, the toxins from our past that made us toxic will be flushed out of our spirits. God desires your spirit to be toxic-free. You can't be a toxic filled Christian if you want to fulfill the call and purpose of God. That's like trying to mix water & oil. Impossible! They don't mix. So I encourage you today to examine your circle. Do those in your circle edify or tear down? Do they talk in secret about each other? Is it a circle of gossipers or a circle of people encouraging those who are down? If you're ready for a healthy spiritual journey with Christ, the first big step is to get rid of the toxins in your circle. It will be the best thing you do. You will notice a difference just like you do after the toxins are flushed out of your physical body.

"I was brought forth in [a state of] wickedness; in sin my mother conceived me [and from my beginning I, too, was sinful]. Behold, you desire truth in the innermost being, and in the hidden part [of my heart] You will make me know wisdom. Purify me with hyssop, and I will be clean; Wash me, and I will be whiter than snow" (Psalm 51:5-7, AMP).

Prayer

Father,

Thank You for purifying me with Your hyssop, so I can be cleansed of any toxins in my spirit. Thank You for washing my heart and my mind, so I can be more and more like You. Reveal if anyone in my circle is causing my spirit to become toxic because toxins aren't healthy for my spirit-man. I cannot win souls for You effectively with them in my spirit. I pray against the Enemy who would make me want to have toxic people in my surroundings. I pray that I won't attract toxic people unless they are specific assignments from You. Thank You for the growth and maturity that awaits me as I begin to drink of the Living Water to flush any toxins from my spirit as I go through life.

Amen!

Additional Prayer Points

_____

_____

_____

_____

_____

_____

_____

_____

_____

_____

_____

Reflection

While reading, what stood out to you? What are some things you heard or felt God was saying? What are your key takeaways & how do you plan to apply them to your daily life, or in the future?

_____
_____
_____
_____
_____
_____
_____
_____
_____
_____
_____
_____
_____
_____
_____
_____
_____
_____
_____
_____
_____
_____
_____
_____
_____
_____
_____
_____

Day Forty-One

One night, I had a vivid dream that I was at the crucifixion of Jesus when the Romans put the crown of thorns on His head (the crown representing royalty & the thorns representing sin) while yelling, "Hail, King of the Jews," mocking Jesus (Matthew 27:29). When I woke up, I wondered why God showed me this dream. It was during a particular time I received the call of God on my life, but I was nervous, intimidated, and afraid to publicly tell people, even family about the calling. Then God led me to Romans 14:11, which says, *"It is written: 'As surely as I live,' says the Lord, 'every knee will bow before me; every tongue will acknowledge God.'"* I asked Him exactly what that meant because I didn't fully understand what He was trying to tell me. I read it again. After I read it for the second and third time, God told me people will talk about, try to humiliate, mock, or even bring up lies and past sins about me publicly. However, I should let them talk because, at the end of the day, they must still acknowledge the call on my life and who God said I am.

So, if you are in a position in life where you a beginning to walk in the call of God or even in obedience to something He told you to do, know everyone won't support you. Some people will talk about and even lie on you to try to strip you of something they didn't have the power to give in the first place, and that's okay. The Enemy will even try to bring up your past to make you weak and turn away from being obedient. But God will strengthen you in those moments and surround you with people who will pray and push you in the direction He wants to take you. So, remember in the end, as long as you are faithful to God and His plan for your life, people will still have to respect and acknowledge what God has said and proclaimed about you!

> *"Indeed, all who delight in pursuing righteousness and are determined to live godly lives in Christ Jesus will be hunted and persecuted [because of their faith]" (2 Timothy 3:12, AMP).*

Prayer

Father,

Thank You for always affirming me when I can't even affirm myself. I thank You for being there when people persecute me and talk down to me because I am being obedient to what You have told me to do. Strengthen me in the moments I feel weak and want to give up. Help me turn away from the voices of the Enemy that will try to bring up my past or even my present fears to stop me from walking in obedience. I pray against the Enemy. He will not make me timid. I will walk in full obedience to my call and the authority You have destined for me to walk in. Surround me with people who will push, pray, and love me when I'm down, not kick me to the curb. Thank You that even though people may talk, lie, and not support what I'm doing for the kingdom, they must still acknowledge who You say I am.

Amen!

Additional Prayer Points

_____

_____

_____

_____

_____

_____

_____

_____

_____

Reflection

While reading, what stood out to you? What are some things you heard or felt God was saying? What are your key takeaways & how do you plan to apply them to your daily life, or in the future?

_____

_____

_____

_____

_____

_____

_____

_____

_____

_____

_____

_____

_____

_____

_____

_____

_____

_____

_____

_____

_____

_____

_____

_____

_____

Day Forty-Two

Sometimes you may feel your "yes" in obedience to God is in vain, but it is not! God's plan is to prosper you and not to harm you in any way. That even goes when you second guess His plan after obeying what He has told you to do. God is not a man that He should lie. Yes, people don't see your private time with God. They don't see those nights when you want to give up on the call or being obedient to His instructions. It may seem hard when people aren't receptive to you pouring into them or God's calling for you to do something that doesn't make sense. Remember, whether it makes sense to you or not, don't lose faith. If you find yourself getting weary or it feels as if the process is longer than expected, don't give up. Don't lose your faith. Trust in God! As long as you are *fully* obedient to His direction and instruction, your "yes" will never be in vain!

"Trust in and rely confidently on the Lord with all your heart and do not rely on your own insight or understanding. In all your ways know and acknowledge and recognize Him, And He will make your paths straight and smooth [removing obstacles that block your way]." (Proverbs 3:5-6, AMP)

Prayer

Father,

Thank You for always pushing me to keep going when I felt my "yes" to a God that never lies or makes mistake was in vain. Forgive me for never fully trusting Your plan and purpose for my life. Although the process of getting to the glory may not be easy, You always put me through situations to change me and my perspective. Help me to continue to obey what You have told me to do even when people aren't receptive, when they are difficult to lead and want to do their own thing. Thank You for strengthening me to press toward the mark when I wanted to give up on my calling and walk of obedience. I pray against the Enemy who will try to come when I'm at my lowest point to make me give up on the call. Give me the faith to know that all things work together for good so when things don't go right or my way, You still plan to use it for good.

Amen!

Additional Prayer Points

_____

_____

_____

_____

_____

_____

_____

_____

Reflection

While reading, what stood out to you? What are some things you heard or felt God was saying? What are your key takeaways & how do you plan to apply them to your daily life, or in the future?

_____
_____
_____
_____
_____
_____
_____
_____
_____
_____
_____
_____
_____
_____
_____
_____
_____
_____
_____
_____
_____
_____
_____
_____
_____
_____

Day Forty-Three

Anyone who has been to a chiropractor knows after the slight pain and fatigue during your first couple of appointments, the therapy is a blessing in the long run. On your first appointment, you circle everywhere you are having problems and the chiropractor will begin to treat the areas that are out of alignment based on the x-ray he takes. It is the same way in our spiritual lives. We have experiences that may cause us to be out of alignment with God's Word, as well as His way and purpose for our lives. We must allow Him to readjust the places He sees are out of alignment.

At times, we must be vulnerable and let God know where or what we want Him to adjust, just as we do with the chiropractor when we circle the problematic areas. Sometimes the reason you are still hurting in your heart, mind, and soul from your past is because you haven't been honest with God. You have not asked Him to help you heal and be realigned in the places that hurt. So I encourage you as you go through your spiritual journey, learn to lean on the ultimate chiropractor: Jesus. Continue to dive into His Word. Have quiet times with Him and seek Him for healing and alignment to His will. The healing process won't always be easy, but through God's strength, we can be completely healed, readjusted, and realigned where we need it the most. Therefore, we can be successful at everything God has called us to do and be!

"Your word is a lamp to my feet and a light to my path. I am greatly afflicted; Renew and revive me [giving me life], O Lord, according to Your word" (Psalm 119:105,107, AMP)

Prayer

Father,

Thank You for realigning and readjusting me in the places I need it most. Thank You for healing and making me whole! Help me to understand this process won't be easy, but Your strength is always made perfect in my weakness. Continue to help me through my spiritual journey when I experience hard seasons that may cause me to come out of alignment with Your Word, will, and way for my life. Help me to stay in alignment with You, but also surround me with people who will hold me accountable and not allow me to rebel against You. Instead, they will chastise me in love when I'm wrong and not operating in the things You have called me to do.

Amen!

Additional Prayer Points

_____

_____

_____

_____

_____

_____

_____

_____

_____

_____

_____

_____

Reflection

While reading, what stood out to you? What are some things you heard or felt God was saying? What are your key takeaways & how do you plan to apply them to your daily life, or in the future?

_____

_____

_____

_____

_____

_____

_____

_____

_____

_____

_____

_____

_____

_____

_____

_____

_____

_____

_____

_____

_____

_____

_____

_____

_____

_____

_____

Day Forty-Four

Sometimes pride can become a hindrance to complete healing in certain seasons of your life. You may go through situations that leave you bitter, angry, and sometimes vengeful. However, God doesn't allow you to conquer seasons in life for you to get revenge, stay bitter or angry at the people who hurt you. Often times, God will use the hurt and pain caused by someone close to you to mature you and change your perspective about certain things. In doing so, you will be cognizant of how you treat other people. Usually, you will need to be the bigger person to lay your pride aside, talk about your differences with that person, and forgive him or her, so you can move on and receive the complete healing you need. You may be the younger one to initiate the conversation, but that doesn't mean you can't be the bigger person. You won't be able to walk in your full potential if you are trying to prove points to people who hurt you. Truth be told, they could care less what you're doing. So stop wasting your energy. Forgive, grow, and move on!

> *"Do not repay anyone evil for evil. Be careful to do what is right in the eyes of everyone. Live in harmony with one another. Do not be proud but be willing to associate with people of low position. Do not be conceited. If it is possible, as far as it depends on you, live at peace with everyone. Do not take revenge, my dear friends, but leave room for God's wrath, for it is written: "It is mine to avenge; I will repay," says the Lord" (Romans 12:16-19, NIV).*

Prayer

Father,

Thank You for sticking by my side through seasons where I was mishandled and mistreated. Thank You for letting me conquer those seasons, so I can be more aware of how I treat people but also to grow and mature me. I pray that when You lead me to talk out my differences with someone that I act in obedience. That way, I can heal. Help me not to be prideful, hold grudges, try to get back at others or prove something to those who have hurt me in the past. Vengeance is Yours. Trying to prove something to people creates pride, and Your Word says You resist the proud. Thank You that in every situation I can be the bigger person, not to be seen, but to be the example You have called me to be.

Amen!

Additional Prayer Points

_____

_____

_____

_____

_____

_____

_____

_____

_____

_____

_____

Reflection

While reading, what stood out to you? What are some things you heard or felt God was saying? What are your key takeaways & how do you plan to apply them to your daily life, or in the future?

_____

_____

_____

_____

_____

_____

_____

_____

_____

_____

_____

_____

_____

_____

_____

_____

_____

_____

_____

_____

_____

_____

_____

_____

_____

_____

_____

_____

Day Forty-Five

You can't expect God to do "exceedingly and abundantly" when you continue to limit and box Him into your traditions, customs, norms, and what He did or how He did it. God is calling you to a new standard! A new standard in worship, prayer, lifestyle, discipline, mindset, stewardship and even devotion to Him. In this season, God is calling you to put away old traditions, customs, norms, what He did and how He did it back then. He wants you to step into His new thing and new way. He desires to do more in your ministry, quiet time with Him, and your time of worship. God is waiting for you, but it is up to you to trust Him and meet Him where He is now. Don't stay where He was.

"Here I am! I stand at the door and knock. If anyone hears my voice and opens the door, I will come in and eat with that person, and they with me" (Revelation 3:20, NIV).

Prayer

Father,

Thank You for the new standard You have released. I pray if I haven't met You where You are and have limited You to where you were, that You would open my heart to Your new standard of worship, devotion, and ministry in my life. I pray that as I meet You where you are that brand new revelation, healing, opportunities, and deliverance will happen like never before. Forgive me for boxing You into the norm, traditions and customs of things. Allow Your Spirit to take over my life and lead me in the new standard You have released. I pray against the Enemy who will attempt to keep me complacent where I am because I am comfortable and used to being where You were. Make me confident about living up to Your standards.

Amen!

Additional Prayer Points

_____

_____

_____

_____

_____

_____

_____

_____

_____

_____

Reflection

While reading, what stood out to you? What are some things you heard or felt God was saying? What are your key takeaways & how do you plan to apply them to your daily life, or in the future?

_____
_____
_____
_____
_____
_____
_____
_____
_____
_____
_____
_____
_____
_____
_____
_____
_____
_____
_____
_____
_____
_____
_____
_____
_____
_____

Day Forty-Six

There's a difference between complacency and contentment. In some seasons of your life, God will teach you to be content (being at peace) about a thing, place, or moment. However, be careful in those seasons that your contentment doesn't become complacency (being satisfied to the point you feel a sense of false security and you don't have to try). Often times, God will keep us in certain seasons to teach us how to wait. He will also do so to mature us in the things we've prayed for or He has told us to wait on. In those seasons, we may become content, which can be a good thing until the Enemy causes us to become complacent and even stagnant. It is not God's will for us to be complacent and stagnant, especially when He is trying to prepare us for future blessings. So if you find yourself in a waiting period of your life, don't give up! Don't allow the Enemy to move you from contentment to complacency and stagnancy. Continue to be at peace in the season you are in, learn what you need to, so you can pass the test and move to the next assignment God has for you.

"And patience produces character, and character produces hope. And this hope will never disappoint us, because God has poured out his love to fill our hearts. He gave us his love through the Holy Spirit, whom God has given to us" (Romans 5:4-5, NCV).

Prayer

Father,

Thank You for every season I had to wait and be patient. I pray that when I come into another season where I have to wait to see the manifestation of something that I will continue to be faithful, fruitful, and content in my season. May I not be complacent while in my season of waiting. I pray against the spirit of stagnation that will come to make me stagnant and steer me away from You and doing Your will while I wait. Thank You that patience produces character, so every time I have to wait You are building my character and faith in You. At the end of the day, no matter how long I have to wait on something, You said it will come to past. You do not lie.

Amen!

Additional Prayer Points

_____

_____

_____

_____

_____

_____

_____

_____

_____

_____

_____

_____

Reflection

While reading, what stood out to you? What are some things you heard or felt God was saying? What are your key takeaways & how do you plan to apply them to your daily life, or in the future?

_____

_____

_____

_____

_____

_____

_____

_____

_____

_____

_____

_____

_____

_____

_____

_____

_____

_____

_____

_____

_____

_____

_____

_____

Day Forty-Seven

On your spiritual journey with God, faith/trust, and patience go hand in hand. God is sovereign, which means He's all-knowing. He knows when you aren't ready for what you have asked. Sometimes, He will give you what you asked for to prove you aren't ready for it. God leads us through seasons of waiting to build our characters, faith in Him, and even our expectations of Him. He has given you certain dreams, visions, prophecies, and words but sometimes it feels as if they are taking too long to manifest. It's not that He isn't going to do it, but He knows that in certain seasons of your life, you can get the right blessing at the wrong time. It's really easy to say you trust God on the good days, but it seems even harder to have the same amount of faith in bad seasons or seasons when He tells you to wait. Remember waiting isn't a punishment but a blessing. God would rather give you the right blessing at the right time than give you a blessing at the wrong time that is too big to handle or one your character or faith isn't ready to deal with.

> *"Wait for and confidently expect the Lord; be strong and let your heart take courage; yes, wait for and confidently expect the Lord"* *(Psalm 27:14, AMP)*

Prayer

Father,

Thank You for every time I had to wait on certain blessings. I know You aren't a man that You should lie or repent, so I thank You every word that comes out of Your mouth is true and won't return to You void. As I wait for my blessing, increase my faith and expectation in You and help me to seek You more, so I can know Your heart better to be more like You. I pray against the Enemy who will come to make me bitter at You or even those around me who are being blessed. Help me to rejoice because I know if You are blessing my neighbors around me, You are in the neighborhood!

Amen!

Additional Prayer Points

_____

_____

_____

_____

_____

_____

_____

_____

_____

_____

_____

Reflection

While reading, what stood out to you? What are some things you heard or felt God was saying? What are your key takeaways & how do you plan to apply them to your daily life, or in the future?

_____

_____

_____

_____

_____

_____

_____

_____

_____

_____

_____

_____

_____

_____

_____

_____

_____

_____

_____

_____

_____

_____

_____

_____

_____

_____

_____

Day Forty-Eight

In life, God may show you certain dreams and visions, but you realize you don't have the qualifications, tools, or money necessary to fulfill them. When God gives you a vision, He will also release the provision needed as long as You obey the vision or dream He has given You! If God gave it to you, no matter what it is, how big or small or how much it costs, He *will* complete it (Philippians 1:6). Therefore, whatever dreams or visions you have been sitting on because you lack the qualifications, tools, money, or even support, write them down. Then pray, seek, and ask God for guidance on how to fulfill what He has given you. When He gives you strategies, write them down. Make the effort and take action to bring the vision and dream into full manifestation.

> *"I am convinced and confident of this very thing, that He who has begun a good work in you will [continue to] perfect and complete it until the day of Christ Jesus [the time of His return]" (Philippians 1:6, AMP).*

Prayer

Father,

Thank You for every dream and vision You have given me. Thank You for trusting me enough as Your son/daughter to carry my dreams and visions to completion with Your help. Thank You that through You, I have everything I need to bring this dream and vision to fruition, and it will be exactly how You want it to be. I pray that as You continue to give me dreams and visions, I will be obedient to the way You want things done and the strategy to complete them. I pray against the Enemy who will make me become tired and weary when it feels as if things are getting hard and not going the right way. I thank You for lifting a standard against the Enemy. Thank You that he will not succeed in making me feel I am lacking the capacity to fulfill the dream or vision You have told me to fulfill.

Amen!

Additional Prayer Points

_____

_____

_____

_____

_____

_____

_____

_____

_____

Reflection

While reading, what stood out to you? What are some things you heard or felt God was saying? What are your key takeaways & how do you plan to apply them to your daily life, or in the future?

_____

_____

_____

_____

_____

_____

_____

_____

_____

_____

_____

_____

_____

_____

_____

_____

_____

_____

_____

_____

_____

_____

_____

_____

_____

_____

_____

Day Forty-Nine

God will put us in certain situations and seasons in life where we have literally done everything in our own strength and the only thing left to do is pray, have faith, and believe God will work it out! Sometimes, He is simply waiting for us to stop acting in our strength when situations are out of our control. He is the only one who can fix it. Often times we worry ourselves sick, stress ourselves out, and even weigh ourselves down because we carry the weight that isn't ours to begin with. God gives us assurance through His Word that if we ask anything by faith in His name according to His will, He will do it! Therefore, no matter what situation you find yourself in, you can overcome. Nothing is too big or small for our God! The weight of worry, stress, doubt, and fear should be given to God because He cares. We should trust that He will provide everything we need!

> *"Cast all your anxiety on him because he cares for you. Humble yourselves, therefore, under God's mighty hand, that he may lift you up in due time" (1 Peter 5:6-7, NIV).*

Prayer

Father,

Thank You I don't have to operate in my strength when in reality, I'm weak inside. I don't have to do this because Your strength is made perfect in our weakness and You care so much for us that when we need anything and ask for it in faith, You grant it for us. I thank You for granting the things we need even though we are too prideful to ask for them sometimes. Help us not to be prideful. Let us be more vulnerable to You because You already know what we need, but we should always be humble enough to still ask our Father in faith for the things we need. I pray against the Enemy who will try to manipulate my mind and make me operate in my strength causing me to be weary and lose faith. I thank You for continuing to provide my every need. Because I am connected to You, I shall not want!

Amen!

Additional Prayer Points

_____

_____

_____

_____

_____

_____

_____

_____

_____

Reflection

While reading, what stood out to you? What are some things you heard or felt God was saying? What are your key takeaways & how do you plan to apply them to your daily life, or in the future?

_____

_____

_____

_____

_____

_____

_____

_____

_____

_____

_____

_____

_____

_____

_____

_____

_____

_____

_____

_____

_____

_____

_____

_____

Day Fifty

You may be in a time of your life when you feel defeated. You can't catch a break, and you feel alone, but God is saying that restoration is coming soon. Everything you've gone through to get you to where you are right now is in His divine plan for a divine purpose. Many times, the Enemy will try to manipulate your mind and make you think God has forgotten about you and left you to fend for yourself, but that is not so! Sometimes, God will put you through the pressures and fire of life to come out with a testimony and to shine like a diamond after it's put through the fire. You will never truly appreciate the blessings, opportunities, and mountaintop experiences God grants you if you never experience, embrace, and learn while in the valley.

> *"After you have suffered for a little while, the God of all grace [who imparts His blessing and favor], who called you to His own eternal glory in Christ, will Himself complete, confirm, strengthen, and establish you [making you what you ought to be]" (1 Peter 5:10, AMP).*

Prayer

Father,

Thank You for every moment in life I had to suffer. I know that since I'm in Christ, I must also suffer like Christ sometimes. Thank You for the ups and downs of life, because those are the things that shape me, my testimony, and anointing into what we are today. I pray against the Enemy who will make me think You have neglected me and make me question Your love for me. I thank You for the restoration that is coming to my life in the places I need it. I also thank You that You loved me so much to send Your Son to die on the cross for me before the foundation of the world. Continue to reveal Your purpose for my life as I seek You and Your righteousness.

Amen!

Additional Prayer Points

_____

_____

_____

_____

_____

_____

_____

_____

_____

_____

_____

Reflection

While reading, what stood out to you? What are some things you heard or felt God was saying? What are your key takeaways & how do you plan to apply them to your daily life, or in the future?

_____

_____

_____

_____

_____

_____

_____

_____

_____

_____

_____

_____

_____

_____

_____

_____

_____

_____

_____

_____

_____

_____

_____

_____

_____

_____

_____

Day Fifty-One

If you are a cook or like to eat, you know what olive oil is made from or how real grape juice is made. In the process of making both, each fruit must go through a pressing or crushing phase to get what we need from it. It is the same in your spiritual journey. Sometimes, God will allow you to go through a season of pressing, shaking, and crushing to pull and birth your potential, which you know you have, but you are too reluctant to use. God will use the very thing you think is trying to take you out during a crushing and pressing season for His glory, as well as your growth and anointing. If you ever find yourself in a season where you feel you have been suffocated, and you are ready to give up, keep pushing! The season may be unbearable, but don't allow the Enemy to convince you to give up! On the other side is the anointing oil and glory of God, which He wants to release in your life.

> *"I consider that our present sufferings are not worth comparing with the glory that will be revealed in us"* *(Romans 8:18, NIV).*

Prayer

Father,

Thank You for every season of crushing and pressing! I thank You that although they may be hard and threaten to kill us that You can and will bring me through. You will bring me out. Give me the tenacity I need to hold on to my faith and Your Word in times of trouble. I know the Enemy will try to make me think otherwise. I rebuke the spirit of fear, anxiety, stress, and death that may linger in these seasons. On the other side of affliction is victory in You, as well as glory, anointing, and oil from You!

Amen!

Additional Prayer Points

_____

_____

_____

_____

_____

_____

_____

_____

_____

_____

_____

Reflection

While reading, what stood out to you? What are some things you heard or felt God was saying? What are your key takeaways & how do you plan to apply them to your daily life, or in the future?

_____

_____

_____

_____

_____

_____

_____

_____

_____

_____

_____

_____

_____

_____

_____

_____

_____

_____

_____

_____

_____

_____

_____

_____

_____

Day Fifty-Two

One night, it was raining torrentially. Thunder rolled and there were lightning strikes. The weather was so severe it woke me out of my sleep. I am a really heavy sleeper so when this happens, the storm is very bad. I tried to pray myself back to sleep. As I started to drift off, the Lord spoke to me and said, "You may be *in* a storm right now, but I've given you the grace to go *through* it because I have *sheltered* you from it!" Sometimes, the Enemy can make you think because you're in a storm you are at risk and unprotected. But as long as you are connected to Jehovah Jireh (the Lord my Provider) and Jehovah Nissi (the Lord our Banner) then you have all the shelter and protection you need. The Lord will lift up a standard against the Enemy during your storm. He will provide shelter for you while you are in it. Therefore, do not fret when you find yourself going through a storm, feel the wind and the waves or see lightning and hear thunder. You are graced to go *through* it, and God is your *shelter* from it!

"Whoever dwells in the shelter of the Most High will rest in the shadow of the Almighty. I will say of the Lord, "He is my refuge and my fortress, my God, in whom I trust." If you say, "The Lord is my refuge," and you make the Most High your dwelling, no harm will overtake you, no disaster will come near your tent" (Psalm 91:1-2, 9-10, NIV).

Prayer

Father,

Thank You for every storm I have faced and will face in my life because I know You are with me. Your rod and staff will comfort me. Thank You for never leaving or forsaking me in times of trouble or happiness. Give me the perseverance I need to go through the storms and pressures of life. I pray that Your strength will uphold me when I'm weak and ready to give up. Thank You for being Jehovah Jireh and Jehovah Nissi; therefore, I am protected from the winds and waves of the storms. I am shielded from the Enemy who will try to get me to quit prematurely.

Amen!

Additional Prayer Points

_____

_____

_____

_____

_____

_____

_____

_____

_____

_____

_____

Reflection

While reading, what stood out to you? What are some things you heard or felt God was saying? What are your key takeaways & how do you plan to apply them to your daily life, or in the future?

_____

_____

_____

_____

_____

_____

_____

_____

_____

_____

_____

_____

_____

_____

_____

_____

_____

_____

_____

_____

_____

_____

_____

_____

_____

_____

Day Fifty-Three

The Enemy loves to attack us when he sees we are most vulnerable. Sometimes, we get so bogged down with the cares of life we operate in our own strength. We try to balance our daily lives, ministries, families, and whatever else we have to manage on our own. When we operate in the strength of our flesh, it only makes us tired and gives the Enemy a portal for manipulation. He will try to attack our minds and bodies. He will try to make us self-sabotage by different addictions we use to cope in our weakest moments. When the Enemy sees he can manipulate you and make you believe his lies, he will try to convince you to give up. However, you must remember the greater the attack, the greater the harvest and testimony thereafter. So if you find yourself in a battle or war with the Enemy, realize you can't operate in the strength of your flesh. You need the strength from our heavenly Father, which is made perfect in our weaknesses. The first step in receiving His strength is to be vulnerable to God.

> *"Three times I pleaded with the Lord to take it away from me. But he said to me, "My grace is sufficient for you, for my power is made perfect in weakness." Therefore, I will boast all the more gladly about my weaknesses, so that Christ's power may rest on me. That is why, for Christ's sake, I delight in weaknesses, in insults, in hardships, in persecutions, in difficulties. For when I am weak, then I am strong" (2 Corinthians 12:8-10, NIV).*

Prayer

Father,

Thank You for the strength You give me through Your Spirit when I am weak. I thank You that even when the Enemy comes to manipulate my mind while I'm down, You lift up a standard against him. I pray that when I feel weak and want to give up, that You will uphold me with Your right hand. Also, surround me with people who will push and encourage me not to stay down, those who will motivate me to get up and keep pushing because on the other side of the test is a testimony, harvest, and blessing.

Amen!

Additional Prayer Points

_____

_____

_____

_____

_____

_____

_____

_____

_____

_____

_____

_____

Reflection

While reading, what stood out to you? What are some things you heard or felt God was saying? What are your key takeaways & how do you plan to apply them to your daily life, or in the future?

_____
_____
_____
_____
_____
_____
_____
_____
_____
_____
_____
_____
_____
_____
_____
_____
_____
_____
_____
_____
_____
_____
_____
_____
_____
_____
_____
_____

Day Fifty-Four

In life, you may look around and feel as though everyone around you is getting a promotion, new house, car, and even getting married. But not you! Sometimes, God will make you wait, not only to make sure you're ready to handle what you desire but to prepare you and increase your level of faith and expectation that God will do it for you. You should always be making preparations in your waiting process. When you go to the doctor, the nurses prep you with a gown and take your vitals to expedite the process. They do this because even though it may seem as if the doctor is seeing everyone else around, when he finally gets to you, he can do what he needs to do, and you can be on your way. Sometimes, preparation is necessary to expedite your process! Yes, people may be getting blessed all around you, but you don't know how long their process took. So while you are waiting, prepare yourself for the blessing(s) you are believing God for and stand in expectation. At any moment, God could be ready to bless you. Therefore, if you ever find yourself waiting on a blessing you see others receiving, don't get discouraged and bitter. Rather, prepare yourself, because your patient preparation will expedite your process!

"Therefore, the Lord waits [expectantly] and longs to be gracious to you, and therefore He waits on high to have compassion on you. For the Lord is a God of justice; blessed (happy, fortunate) are all those who long for Him [since He will never fail them]" (Isaiah 30:18, AMP).

Prayer

Father,

Thank You for every time You made me wait and be patient for what I wanted. Thank You that my patience and preparation for these things will expedite the process when You are ready to bless me! As I see others being blessed help me not to become bitter or allow the Enemy to make me jealous or envious. Help me to be sincerely happy, knowing that if You are blessing my neighbors, it's only a matter of time before You come down my street and stop at my house. I continue to stand in faith and expectation of the blessings coming my way. I will not allow the Enemy to make me settle or become weary in my patience. I will continue to declare Your Word that You long to be gracious to us and those who wait will be blessed because You are a God of justice!

Amen!

Additional Prayer Points

_____

_____

_____

_____

_____

_____

_____

_____

_____

_____

Reflection

While reading, what stood out to you? What are some things you heard or felt God was saying? What are your key takeaways & how do you plan to apply them to your daily life, or in the future?

_____

_____

_____

_____

_____

_____

_____

_____

_____

_____

_____

_____

_____

_____

_____

_____

_____

_____

_____

_____

_____

_____

_____

_____

_____

_____

Day Fifty-Five

When you live a life expecting God's presence, power, anointing, revelation, blessings, miracles, signs, and wonders, He will do more than you can ever fathom. Often times, we don't see God do the extraordinary in our lives or the lives of others because our faith, expectations, and belief in Him to do it aren't in agreement. You can say you believe God to do a thing in your life all day long, but does your faith align with how much you say you believe and expect? God is ready to blow your mind with certain things, but you cannot have an "I'll believe it when I see it" mentality. Your faith, expectation, and belief in Him to do it must align. Otherwise, it negates the entire concept of having faith, hope, and expectation for something because the Bible says in Hebrews 11:1, *"Now faith is the substance of things hoped for, the evidence of things not seen."* Therefore, the things you can't see are the things you must have hope and faith in God to do, expecting He will do it!

"Now to Him who is able to do exceedingly abundantly above all that we ask or think, according to the power that works in us, to Him be glory in the church by Christ Jesus to all generations, forever and ever. Amen" (Ephesians 3:20-21, NKJV).

Prayer

Father,

Thank You for Your ability to do what I can't even begin to ask or think You can do for me! I thank You for being the God who will do the impossible and the unimaginable! As I go through my spiritual journey increase my faith and hope in You. I pray they will be in alignment, so You can do the impossible and unimaginable in my life! Help me to live in expectancy, *daily*! I pray against the Enemy who will try to send things my way to decrease my hope and faith in You! I know You can and will do everything You said You will do in my life. So until I see the manifestation, I stand in faith and expectation.

Amen!

Additional Prayer Points

_____

_____

_____

_____

_____

_____

_____

_____

_____

_____

_____

Reflection

While reading, what stood out to you? What are some things you heard or felt God was saying? What are your key takeaways & how do you plan to apply them to your daily life, or in the future?

_____

_____

_____

_____

_____

_____

_____

_____

_____

_____

_____

_____

_____

_____

_____

_____

_____

_____

_____

_____

_____

_____

_____

_____

_____

Day Fifty-Six

In life, before you can possess something, God will make you get into position for it. Before He speaks to you regarding certain things you've asked for, whether it's strategy, clarity, understanding, vision, or any other specific blessing or petition, you must be in the right position and posture to receive it from Him. Many times, we get out of alignment with what He has told us to do, and He's simply waiting for us to get back into a position and posture of obedience, so we can see what He is saying to us. You may need to go back and finish what He has told you to finish or start what you are reluctant to start because you want to know every detail before you do so. Many times, God will give you the strategy, vision, clarity, and understanding you need from Him on a specific thing when you obey the previous things He has told you to do. Therefore, in the next few days, if you have forgotten, ask God to reveal what you have neglected to do, which has God quiet on a certain matter in your life. Then reposition yourself. You may have to realign your mindset, faith, worship, and devotion, so you do what is necessary to fit into God's plan.

> *"I will take my post; I will position myself on the fortress. I will keep watch to see what the Lord says to me and how he will respond to my complaint" (Habakkuk 2:1, CEB).*

Prayer

Father,

Thank You for being gracious and patient with me when I get out of alignment with Your plan and what You have told me to do. I pray that you continue to chastise me when I get out of alignment with the instructions that have given me. Help me to reposition and posture myself in obedience, so I cannot see and hear what You want to reveal to me. As I posture myself correctly and do the things You have said, give me the clarity, understanding, and knowledge I need and ask for.

Amen!

Additional Prayer Points

_____

_____

_____

_____

_____

_____

_____

_____

_____

_____

_____

_____

_____

Reflection

While reading, what stood out to you? What are some things you heard or felt God was saying? What are your key takeaways & how do you plan to apply them to your daily life, or in the future?

_____

_____

_____

_____

_____

_____

_____

_____

_____

_____

_____

_____

_____

_____

_____

_____

_____

_____

_____

_____

_____

_____

_____

_____

_____

_____

Day Fifty-Seven

Be careful! Do not let the Enemy muzzle you in this season. Don't allow him to make you think God isn't hearing your prayers and petitions to Him. Don't let the Enemy continue to keep You in isolation and quiet in times of worship and praise. Times of worship are the best times to begin to pray and intercede. The Enemy loves to make you think you are living under a closed heaven, but that is not so! God cares. He hears the cries and petitions of His children. We are under an open heaven and whatever you need is in what you speak into the atmosphere according to the will of God. God is waiting, willing, and ready to release many things on your behalf. However, until you stop allowing the Enemy to place a muzzle over you, you will never obtain many of those blessings.

"I assure you and most solemnly say to you, whatever you bind [forbid, declare to be improper and unlawful] on earth shall have [already] been bound in heaven, and whatever you loose [permit, declare lawful] on earth shall have [already] been loosed in heaven" (Matthew 18:18, AMP).

Prayer

Father,

Thank You that I live under an open heaven and You hear and answer prayer! Help me to stop the Enemy from placing a muzzle over my mouth in this season. You desire to give me so many things in the spiritual realm, but I must call them forth by faith. I thank You that whatever I bind and loose on the earth according to Your Word will be bound and loosed in the heavenly realm! I thank You for the authority to call things that I cannot see, into the natural by faith in You!

Amen!

Additional Prayer Points

_____

_____

_____

_____

_____

_____

_____

_____

_____

_____

_____

_____

_____

Reflection

While reading, what stood out to you? What are some things you heard or felt God was saying? What are your key takeaways & how do you plan to apply them to your daily life, or in the future?

_____
_____
_____
_____
_____
_____
_____
_____
_____
_____
_____
_____
_____
_____
_____
_____
_____
_____
_____
_____
_____
_____
_____
_____
_____
_____
_____

Day Fifty-Eight

STOP SECOND GUESSING YOURSELF!

You know what God said concerning that "thing" you continue to worry yourself about, whether it's a job, relationship, a big move, school, or something else! God gave you a sign verbally or otherwise to start the business, apply for the loan for the business, house, school, or grant. He told you to get your credit right and reconcile with that loved one, but you have yet to do it. Have you allowed the Enemy to convince you that it wouldn't work or the risk wouldn't be worth it? Have you allowed the distractions around you to suppress what God has told you to do? Have you allowed the naysayers to talk you out of the things that are not even for them to understand? Or is your faith level so low you have yet to come into agreement with the very thing God said to do or not to do? This act of faith in obedience to God could make a *huge* difference. It can change the trajectory of things for you and generations coming after you!

God is standing on the water telling you to get out of the boat and walk, but you are too busy focusing on the wind and waves God has complete control over. He's saying at this moment, "Why do you doubt? Have faith. Stay focused on Me, not the things going on around you. Come!"

The question is will you continue to stay in your boat of fear, self-doubt, and complacency or will you get out of the boat, walk on the water of fear, be obedient, and trust what God has told you to do?

"But Jesus immediately said to them: "Take courage! It is I. Don't be afraid." "Lord, if it's you," Peter replied, "tell me to come to you on the water." "Come," he said. Then Peter got down out of the boat, walked on the water and came toward Jesus. But when he saw the wind, he was afraid and, beginning to sink, cried out, "Lord, save me!" Immediately Jesus reached out his hand and caught him. "You of little faith," he said, "why did you doubt?"(Matthew 14:27-31, NIV).

Prayer

Father,

Thank You for always affirming me when I doubt myself. I pray You will deliver me from the fear and self-doubt I have. Help me to understand Your Word declares I can do *all things* through Christ who strengthens me! I know if You have called me to do an assignment, You will bring me through it. As I step out in faith on the things You have told me to do, I rebuke the Enemy and the naysayers who will try to make me second-guess myself and what You have said. Build up my faith so that even when I obey You when it looks crazy to other people that the fruit of my obedience will speak for itself. Help me to get out of my boat of fear, self-doubt, and complacency. Help me to trust and have faith in You to never leave me or forsake me.

Amen!

Additional Prayer Points

_____

_____

_____

_____

_____

_____

_____

_____

_____

_____

Reflection

While reading, what stood out to you? What are some things you heard or felt God was saying? What are your key takeaways & how do you plan to apply them to your daily life, or in the future?

_____

_____

_____

_____

_____

_____

_____

_____

_____

_____

_____

_____

_____

_____

_____

_____

_____

_____

_____

_____

_____

_____

_____

_____

_____

_____

_____

Day Fifty-Nine

Many times in life, when you reach a point where you become submitted and obedient to God, the Enemy will try to bring your past up, especially when You have moved past it, asked for forgiveness from God, and have peace about it. It is difficult when the Enemy throws our past in our face to stop us from doing the things of God. Sometimes we allow him to condemn us because although we have forgiveness from God, we neglect to forgive ourselves. If you don't learn how to forgive yourself from the past things you've done, you'll poison your present and ultimately, it can affect your future as well. Therefore, don't let the Enemy hang your past over your head because there is no condemnation to those who are in the Lord. Jesus forgave you through His blood when He died on the cross. Forgive yourself and move on!

"Therefore, if anyone is in Christ, the new creation has come: The old has gone, the new is here! All this is from God, who reconciled us to himself through Christ and gave us the ministry of reconciliation: that God was reconciling the world to himself in Christ, not counting people's sins against them. And he has committed to us the message of reconciliation" (2 Corinthians 5:17-19, NIV).

Prayer

Father,

I thank You that when I accepted You into my life I became a new creature! Thank You that everything in my past has passed away and all things are made new. Therefore, I have a new mind, heart, and future in You! Thank You for forgiving me on Calvary, reconciling us and not counting our sins against us. Even though I may fall short of Your glory, help me not to allow the Enemy or myself to condemn me for the wrong I've done.

Amen!

Additional Prayer Points

_____

_____

_____

_____

_____

_____

_____

_____

_____

_____

_____

_____

Reflection

While reading, what stood out to you? What are some things you heard or felt God was saying? What are your key takeaways & how do you plan to apply them to your daily life, or in the future?

_____

_____

_____

_____

_____

_____

_____

_____

_____

_____

_____

_____

_____

_____

_____

_____

_____

_____

_____

_____

_____

_____

_____

_____

_____

_____

_____

_____

Day Sixty

It is important to know your identity in Christ and not let the Enemy manipulate you into thinking your past or current failures or mistakes are your identity. Stop worrying about the thoughts people have towards you. Sometimes, the Enemy will use that to discourage you and make you give up and quit, especially when you are doing what God has told you to do. Don't let that stop you. Remember your identity in Christ because you are a new creature. Encourage and affirm yourself daily. Keep moving forward. Be free from the bondage of the opinions and whispers of people around you. The best encouragement is the one you receive from yourself. So be careful what you say and put into the atmosphere because the things you say will begin to align your spirit with the words you are saying.

> *"But you are a chosen people, a royal priesthood, a holy nation, God's special possession, that you may declare the praises of him who called you out of darkness into his wonderful light" (1 Peter 2:9, NIV).*

Prayer

Father,

Thank You that when I came into the family of Christ, I became a new creature, and You gave me a new identity. Help me to understand the Enemy will use the whispers of people around me to discourage me and make me want to give up on life and the things You have told me to do. Give me strength when I feel as if I am inadequate and unworthy. Help me to speak the things You have said about me but also surround me with loving people who will pick me up, not kick me while I'm down.

Amen!

Additional Prayer Points

_____

_____

_____

_____

_____

_____

_____

_____

_____

_____

_____

_____

_____

Reflection

While reading, what stood out to you? What are some things you heard or felt God was saying? What are your key takeaways & how do you plan to apply them to your daily life, or in the future?

_____

_____

_____

_____

_____

_____

_____

_____

_____

_____

_____

_____

_____

_____

_____

_____

_____

_____

_____

_____

_____

_____

_____

_____

_____

Day Sixty-One

Some people want to see you doing well as long as you are on the same level as them, whether it's spiritually, physically, mentally, academically, relationally, etc. You must be okay with that understanding, they believe you must limit yourself to that level and go no further. Therefore, always ask God for discernment to reveal those who are jealous or envious of your growth and maturity, especially if they are close to you or in your circle. Many people who are secretly envious of your growth and maturity are the same ones trying to tear you down and defame your character. The Enemy will try to use your complacent friends to discourage you and keep you complacent as well. So make sure to keep people in your circle who sincerely want you to grow and mature, even if that means you outgrow them. Be careful of those in close proximity who are jealous and envious of your growth. They will try to ruin the new things and blessings God has for you because they are bitter instead of growing with you.

"A perverse man spreads strife, and one who gossips separates intimate friends" (Proverbs 16:28, AMP).

Prayer

Father,

I pray and earnestly ask for the gift to discern spirits, so I can spiritually determine the motives of those around me and those I come into contact with. Lord, help me to understand that everyone won't be okay with my growth and maturity, and I have to be okay with that. Give me the strength to let go of the ones who secretly despise me and are jealous and envious of me. I pray against the Enemy who tries to manipulate me and make me believe I should stay complacent to keep friends who are also complacent.

Amen!

Additional Prayer Points

_____

_____

_____

_____

_____

_____

_____

_____

_____

_____

_____

_____

_____

Reflection

While reading, what stood out to you? What are some things you heard or felt God was saying? What are your key takeaways & how do you plan to apply them to your daily life, or in the future?

_____

_____

_____

_____

_____

_____

_____

_____

_____

_____

_____

_____

_____

_____

_____

_____

_____

_____

_____

_____

_____

_____

_____

_____

_____

_____

Day Sixty-Two

There comes a time in your life when you must surround and connect yourself to those striving to walk in obedience to Christ. The Lord longs to bless His children, but especially those who are obedient to what He has said. Many times, you may not be the one to receive the blessing. However, most times, when you are connected to obedient believers, the Lord will allow the overflow from their lives to pour into your life. When you connect to obedient believers, you gain accountability partners who will hold you responsible. They chastise you in love when you are wrong or not living up to God's expectations. After a while, you'll begin to live a life pleasing to God more and more, take on the traits of the Holy Spirit and be an obedient believer. You will walk upright in Christ and holiness.

> *"For the Lord God is a sun and shield; The Lord bestows grace and favor and honor; No good thing will He withhold from those who walk uprightly" (Psalm 84:11, AMP).*

Prayer

Father,

Thank You for surrounding and connecting me those who are striving to walk in obedience to Your will and Word. I thank You that they will hold me accountable when I need it and chastise me when I am wrong. Continue to light a fire in my heart to live how You want me to live and not based on the standards of the world because although I am in the world, I am not of it. Help me to listen and take heed to Your voice and what You say to me. I pray against the Enemy who will send distractions and temptations to make me fall. But although a righteous man may fall 7 times, he will always rise. So help me to rise when I fall for the tactics and temptations of the Enemy. Help me to shun and rebuke evil, so it will flee.

Amen!

Additional Prayer Points

_____

_____

_____

_____

_____

_____

_____

_____

_____

_____

Reflection

While reading, what stood out to you? What are some things you heard or felt God was saying? What are your key takeaways & how do you plan to apply them to your daily life, or in the future?

_____

_____

_____

_____

_____

_____

_____

_____

_____

_____

_____

_____

_____

_____

_____

_____

_____

_____

_____

_____

_____

_____

_____

Day Sixty-Three

Even when you face opposition in life while trying to achieve your goals, do what God has called you to do, or walk in full obedience and faith, do not quit! You aren't facing adversity for something you did. Rather, you're facing it because of the call on your life. Therefore, count it joy when it comes because that means you are heading in the right direction to your purpose. God didn't give you a spirit of fear. The Enemy's job is to instill fear in your spirit as an obstacle to stop you from achieving. His job is to steal your joy, kill your faith in God, and destroy your identity. You need to understand God did not place you on the earth to back down when the Enemy comes to make you quit. In fact, the Lord gave you power over the Enemy! The Word of God in Luke 10:19 tells us, *"Behold, I have given you authority to tread upon serpents and scorpions, and over all the power of the enemy: and nothing shall in any wise hurt you."* Therefore, when the Enemy sends adversity your way to stop you, God not only gave you the power to defeat him but to tread all over him. So the next time you face adversity, declare your power over the Enemy. Walk over him and declare the victory!

"For God has not given us a spirit of fear, but of power and of love and of a sound mind" (2 Timothy 1:7, NKJV).

Prayer

Father,

Thank You for not giving me the spirit of fear or timidity! Help me to tap into the power, love, and sound mind You granted me, so when the Enemy and adversity come, I will not only defeat them but walk over them. Thank You for adversity. It is a good thing when it comes because I know I am headed in the right direction. Adversity is the Enemy's way of stopping me from getting closer to my destiny and operating in my call and purpose for my life. Help me to remember I have the power over the Enemy. He is a defeated foe, so when he does come, I won't back down but operate in the full power You have given me.

Amen!

Additional Prayer Points

_____

_____

_____

_____

_____

_____

_____

_____

_____

_____

_____

Reflection

While reading, what stood out to you? What are some things you heard or felt God was saying? What are your key takeaways & how do you plan to apply them to your daily life, or in the future?

_____

_____

_____

_____

_____

_____

_____

_____

_____

_____

_____

_____

_____

_____

_____

_____

_____

_____

_____

_____

_____

_____

_____

_____

_____

_____

_____

_____

_____

Day Sixty-Four

Sometimes in your life, you may become weak and worn. You may feel as if you don't have the strength to pray for yourself to come out from where you are. However, God always places someone or people around you to spiritually cover and pray for you, whether you know it or not. You are even surviving off the prayers of those who you don't even associate with. Often times, God will place people in your circle or in association with you to simply pray and encourage you, as well as bring you out of dark places you may find yourself in. Don't take it for granted or mistreat those God places in your corner to pray for you! God is always concerned about His children and will do anything He can to prevent them from giving up in times of vulnerability. He will place people around you to pick you up when you're down, encourage you when you want to quit, and love you when you don't have the strength to love yourself. That's the loving, caring, and sovereign heavenly Father we have! He knows what we need and to give us that tough love when we need it the most!

"A friend loves at all times, and a brother is born for adversity" (Proverbs 17:17, AMP).

Prayer

Father,

Thank You for everyone You have assigned to my life to pray for me, even the people I don't directly associate with. I thank You for being concerned about me. I know You will do whatever You must to stop me from giving up in my times of vulnerability! Help me to understand it is the Enemy's job to distract me and try to make me give up in my low seasons. Help me to keep my mind on You because if I do so, You will keep me in perfect peace. I rebuke the spirit of depression, suicidal thoughts, stress, and anxiety that will try to kill me prematurely when I get tired and weak.

Amen!

Additional Prayer Points

_____

_____

_____

_____

_____

_____

_____

_____

_____

_____

_____

_____

Reflection

While reading, what stood out to you? What are some things you heard or felt God was saying? What are your key takeaways & how do you plan to apply them to your daily life, or in the future?

_____

_____

_____

_____

_____

_____

_____

_____

_____

_____

_____

_____

_____

_____

_____

_____

_____

_____

_____

_____

_____

_____

_____

_____

_____

Day Sixty-Five

In life, you must always learn that despite whatever situation or circumstance you may find yourself in, you should still trust and serve God, as well as be humble and faithful to Him. In the Bible, Job was stripped of everything: money, home, and family. Nevertheless, God knew Job would not turn against Him. Often times, we go through life and question why God causes certain things, but that isn't necessarily always the case. Sometimes the Enemy causes things and the Lord permits it to happen to prove a point to the Enemy and you. Job truly didn't realize until after he went through everything he did how much faith and strength he had in God. His adversity built his character and made his faith stronger. It didn't lessen it. In the end, God restored Job with better and double what he had before because of his selflessness in praying for his friends when he had nothing. He was faithful to God and to the process he had to go through. Not only that, God proved to Satan that even though he caused tests and storms to occur in Job's life, he remembered everything his teacher taught him. Therefore, if you find yourself in a season of testing, and you are wondering why the Enemy is attacking you so hard or you blame God for the tests and storms, keep the faith. Continue to humbly serve because on the other side of your perseverance and selflessness is *double and better* than what you had before.

> *"Why should I put myself in danger and take my life in my own hands? Even if God kills me, I have hope in him; I will still defend my ways to his face" (Job 13:14-15, NCV).*

Prayer

Father,

Thank You for never ever leaving my side when I was faced with a storm, test or trial in my life. Thank You for always bringing me through and out of the storm I was in. Help me to increase my faith in the storm and understand that in You, I can do all things. I am more than a conqueror through You. I pray against the Enemy who will try to manipulate my mind and make me think taking myself out is better than persevering through the storms of life. I pray that when I find myself in a storm, I will have a song to calm my heart and settle my spirit. I thank You that even now, You are increasing my faith in You for the next storm I have to face because I know on the other side of my storm is a promise. For my faithfulness and perseverance, You will grant me favor, better, and double for the trouble I had to go through!

Amen!

Additional Prayer Points

_____

_____

_____

_____

_____

_____

_____

_____

_____

Reflection

While reading, what stood out to you? What are some things you heard or felt God was saying? What are your key takeaways & how do you plan to apply them to your daily life, or in the future?

_____
_____
_____
_____
_____
_____
_____
_____
_____
_____
_____
_____
_____
_____
_____
_____
_____
_____
_____
_____
_____
_____
_____
_____
_____
_____

Day Sixty-Six

When God gives you certain visions, dreams, and ideas, sometimes it's not for everyone to know because they don't have the capacity and faith to understand, but you must be okay with that! You'll find it easier to fulfill your dreams and visions when you get rid of the negative people around you who spectate everything you share with them about what God has shown you. The hard truth is everything God gives you isn't to be shared with everyone. It is easy for dream killers to detour and distract you from finishing the thing(s) God has told you to do. This happens, especially when they don't have the faith or simply aren't able to comprehend it. You must be okay with working diligently and silently in some seasons. Let your fruit speak for you!

"Therefore, my dear brothers and sisters, stand firm. Let nothing move you. Always give yourselves fully to the work of the Lord, because you know that your labor in the Lord is not in vain" (1 Corinthians 15:58, NIV).

Prayer

Father,

I thank You for every vision, dream, and idea You have given me to complete. Help me to understand that everyone won't be able to comprehend the things You tell me to do. Help me to do Your will in the seasons of silence. I pray against those in my circle who will try to deter me from completing the assignments You have told me to finish because of their lack of capacity and faith. I also pray against the Enemy who will try to knock me off the course of obedience. Help me to continue to press toward the prize of the Most High calling.

Amen!

Additional Prayer Points

_____

_____

_____

_____

_____

_____

_____

_____

_____

_____

_____

_____

Reflection

While reading, what stood out to you? What are some things you heard or felt God was saying? What are your key takeaways & how do you plan to apply them to your daily life, or in the future?

_____

_____

_____

_____

_____

_____

_____

_____

_____

_____

_____

_____

_____

_____

_____

_____

_____

_____

_____

_____

_____

_____

_____

_____

_____

_____

Day Sixty-Seven

God never permits pain without releasing purpose! In life, you will go through times of heartache and pain. It can get so bad you will question why you are experiencing it. God will use the time of your hardest pain to birth and manifest purpose in you. The pain of your past or present can also hurt so much it may leave a wound. It is important that you take the time to heal mentally, physically, and spiritually because it's always during the healing and restoration process that you find purpose. God will permit seasons of sickness, depression, abuse, etc., in your life to help others who are going or have been through what you have conquered. It may be hard, but your pain is for a reason and a season, so don't despise it. If you wonder what your purpose is, reflect on your past pain because most likely, that's where purpose lies.

> *"Not only so, but we also glory in our sufferings, because we know that suffering produces perseverance; perseverance, character; and character, hope" (Romans 5:3-4, NIV).*

Prayer

Father,

As hard as it may have been, thank You for every difficult season of pain and suffering I had to go through. I know everything You do has a purpose. Hence, the pain and suffering I had to endure had purpose in them as well. Help and strengthen me in those seasons when it is hard to persevere, endure, and be faithful. Even though the Enemy will try to manipulate my mind during this season, I know You will uphold me with Your right hand and never leave me or forsake me. Help me to heal from any internal or spiritual wounds the pain may have caused. Help me to find the purpose You birthed from the pain I had to go through. Help me to use my testimony of breakthrough and healing to help and heal someone else.

Amen!

Additional Prayer Points

_____

_____

_____

_____

_____

_____

_____

_____

_____

_____

Reflection

While reading, what stood out to you? What are some things you heard or felt God was saying? What are your key takeaways & how do you plan to apply them to your daily life, or in the future?

_____

_____

_____

_____

_____

_____

_____

_____

_____

_____

_____

_____

_____

_____

_____

_____

_____

_____

_____

_____

_____

_____

_____

_____

_____

Day Sixty-Eight

Many times in life, you may get discouraged about your purpose or even finding what it is. Finding your purpose won't be easy. You will go through a lot of pain, tests, and trials to discover what it is. Many people don't find their purpose at the same time; some find it in college, after graduation, or even in their 50s and 60s, so don't compare yourself to others who know and are operating in theirs. The most important thing about finding purpose is staying in the face of God and seeking *His* purpose for Your life. Often times, we may try to operate in the purpose we want for our lives and realize it is hard to do so; that's God's way of letting you know it isn't your purpose. Seek and ask God daily for your purpose in life and in due time, He will begin to manifest it; sometimes without you even knowing. He will send people to confirm it or even reveal it to you Himself. Therefore, always be alert and listening. When you begin to walk in obedience and the purpose of God, life won't become peaches and cream, but you will know you are in the right place!

"Though I walk in the midst of trouble, you preserve my life; you stretch out your hand against the wrath of my enemies, and your right hand delivers me. The Lord will fulfill his purpose for me; your steadfast love, O Lord, endures forever. Do not forsake the work of your hands"(Psalm 138:7-8, ESV).

Prayer

Father,

Thank You for everything I have to go through to find my purpose in You. I thank You for creating me for a specific plan and purpose. Help me to find what that is, so I can operate in it fully. I pray that when I find my purpose, I will fulfill it to the best of my ability. Help me to be obedient while I do so, not in the flesh but always in the spirit. I pray against the Enemy who would come to deter me from operating in my full potential and purpose in life and even try to make me stagnant and complacent where I am. Help me not to compare myself to others who have found their purpose because I know the race isn't for the swift. Light a fire in me daily to seek Your face for what You want me to fulfill in Your kingdom. Preserve my life as I do so.

Amen!

Additional Prayer Points

_____

_____

_____

_____

_____

_____

_____

_____

_____

_____

Reflection

While reading, what stood out to you? What are some things you heard or felt God was saying? What are your key takeaways & how do you plan to apply them to your daily life, or in the future?

_____

_____

_____

_____

_____

_____

_____

_____

_____

_____

_____

_____

_____

_____

_____

_____

_____

_____

_____

_____

_____

_____

_____

_____

_____

_____

_____

_____

_____

_____

Day Sixty-Nine

The hardest time in life is when you are going through a season of testing, and it feels as though God has forsaken you and isn't hearing or answering your prayers. But that is not the case. When you are going through tests, it may seem like God has turned a deaf ear on your prayers and cries, but He is actually being silent because a teacher never talks during the test. God never leaves or forsakes His children, but He will remain silent while you're in a season of testing. Many times, the Enemy will make you think the test you are going through is torment, but it's not. God will allow tests to come your way to let you see where your faith and authority lies, how well you can handle the pressure connected to the next level, and to ultimately promote you. Often times, you may give up in your test because you allow the Enemy to torment and distract you. You may even allow those around you to shift your focus while in your test. Remember, when you are being tested, God has already instilled in you everything you need to know for your test. It takes the pressure of tests and storms to pull it out. If He sees you are ready for the next level of glory, God will grant you favor and move you up higher. Don't allow the Enemy to torment you and make you give up prematurely during a test!

> *"Blessed is the man who remains steadfast under trial, for when he has stood the test, he will receive the crown of life, which God has promised to those who love him" (James 1:12, ESV).*

Prayer

Father,

Thank You for every test I have been through because I know that in order to be elevated, I must be tested. I pray that as I continue on my spiritual journey, You will prepare and equip me with the things I need to successfully pass every test. Help me to understand that even if I don't pass the first time, Your grace and mercy will always allow me to retest! I pray against the Enemy who will try to torment me during a testing season and make me feel as though You have forsaken me. I know You will never leave me or forsake me. I thank You for the victory over the Enemy and every test I am put through from today forward.

Amen!

Additional Prayer Points

_____

_____

_____

_____

_____

_____

_____

_____

_____

_____

Reflection

While reading, what stood out to you? What are some things you heard or felt God was saying? What are your key takeaways & how do you plan to apply them to your daily life, or in the future?

_____

_____

_____

_____

_____

_____

_____

_____

_____

_____

_____

_____

_____

_____

_____

_____

_____

_____

_____

_____

_____

_____

_____

_____

Day Seventy

Many times in life you may be in a rough situation and don't know how things will work out or if it will ever change. However, God has given you the authority and power to speak to your situation and bring about change by faith! God lives in us, and we must speak things according to His will that align with what He has said. So, if you find yourself in sickness, fear, bondage, lack, etc., know that those are not a part of God or the heirs of His kingdom. Learn to speak in faith what God has said about your situations. Say you are rich, healed, delivered, and unafraid. Your situation must and will begin to align to the Word of God. Faith is all you need to speak in the authority and power God has given you. So no longer will you allow the Enemy to make you wallow in your ungodly situation!

> *"And Jesus answered them, "Have faith in God. Truly, I say to you, whoever says to this mountain, 'Be taken up and thrown into the sea,' and does not doubt in his heart, but believes that what he says will come to pass, it will be done for him. Therefore, I tell you, whatever you ask in prayer, believe that you have received it, and it will be yours. And whenever you stand praying, forgive, if you have anything against anyone, so that your Father also who is in heaven may forgive you your trespasses" (Mark 11:22-25, ESV).*

Prayer

Father,

I thank You for the power and authority You have given me to speak to my situations through faith. I thank You that because I can speak what You have spoken, any situation that is not like You *must* change. Help me truly understand how much power my words have. I know Proverbs 18:21 says, *"Death & life lie in the power of the tongue."* Therefore, help me to use my words wisely! I pray against the Enemy who will cause me to lose faith and my identity in You. He wants to keep me bound in the situation I want to be delivered from. I thank You for always hearing and performing. Even though it's not always in my time, I will anxiously and patiently wait with expectation, knowing my breakthrough is on the way.

Amen!

Additional Prayer Points

_____

_____

_____

_____

_____

_____

_____

_____

_____

_____

Reflection

While reading, what stood out to you? What are some things you heard or felt God was saying? What are your key takeaways & how do you plan to apply them to your daily life, or in the future?

_____

_____

_____

_____

_____

_____

_____

_____

_____

_____

_____

_____

_____

_____

_____

_____

_____

_____

_____

_____

_____

_____

_____

_____

_____

_____

_____

Day Seventy-One

The Enemy attempts to cloud your life with negative thoughts, mindsets, and people who will hinder you from doing the things God has told you to do. The Enemy hates to see when you are striving to do the right thing, being obedient, productive, and proactive. When he tempts, distracts, and uses negative people to come your way, count it joy because you know you are headed in the right direction. But use spiritual discernment and make sure you don't entertain the things assigned to entice and entangle you. The Enemy wants to see you trapped in bondage, shame, fear, condemnation, and so much more. His aim is to stop you from fulfilling everything God has called you to do and be. As long as you are using spiritual discernment of spirits to test the motives of the people who try to enter your life or the temptations the Enemy sends to entice and entangle you, you'll be able to shun evil. It will flee from you.

> *"So, submit to [the authority of] God. Resist the devil [stand firm against him] and he will flee from you" (James 4:7, AMP).*

Prayer

Father,

Thank You that it is a good sign when the Enemy is throwing temptation and negativity my way to stop me from moving closer to You and fulfilling my call and purpose. Help me to continue to shun and resist the evil temptations and negativity that come to cloud my mind or entangle me in the bondage of the Enemy. If I am entertaining the Enemy in any shape form or fashion, deliver me from it in Jesus' name. Give me spiritual discernment and reveal the negative, toxic people the Enemy sends my way to impede my progress. I know I have a purpose in You and the Enemy wants to do everything he can to stop it, so give me the strength to ignore him and his motives.

Amen!

Additional Prayer Points

_____

_____

_____

_____

_____

_____

_____

_____

_____

_____

_____

_____

Reflection

While reading, what stood out to you? What are some things you heard or felt God was saying? What are your key takeaways & how do you plan to apply them to your daily life, or in the future?

_____
_____
_____
_____
_____
_____
_____
_____
_____
_____
_____
_____
_____
_____
_____
_____
_____
_____
_____
_____
_____
_____
_____
_____
_____
_____

Day Seventy-Two

Many times in your life, God will deliver you from certain situations, but you will allow the Enemy to make you run back to them. It could be an addiction, mindset, or even people. The Enemy's job is to impede your progress. When God delivers you from a certain thing that could be detrimental to what you hold inside of you means, you become a storm chaser. Storm chasers are people who run after storms and tornadoes as a hobby. That's what can happen on your spiritual journey. God removes things that can be catastrophic to your calling, but you run after them. When you let the Enemy manipulate you into taking them back because you are bored, lonely, angry at the new standard God is holding you to or you "can't live without it," it becomes idolatry and rebellion. One, you are putting it above God, but two, it's like smacking God in the face and telling Him, "I didn't want to be delivered from this, so I'm going back to the thing you removed that will cause danger to me, my calling, and future." If you find yourself in a storm, ask God to reveal if it's a self-influenced storm or an actual storm Satan is using to attack you. God will allow a self-influenced storm to continue, until you stop being rebellious, get back in alignment with Him, and do what He has told you to do. He will always provide a way of escape when you do because of His grace and mercy.

Look at the story of Jonah (Jonah 1) in the Bible:

> *"Go to the great city of Nineveh and preach against it, because its wickedness has come up before me." The word of the Lord came to Jonah son of Amittai: But Jonah ran away from the Lord and headed for Tarshish. He went down to Joppa, where he found a ship bound for that port. After paying the fare, he went aboard and sailed for Tarshish to flee from the Lord. Then the Lord sent a great wind on the sea, and such a violent storm arose that the ship threatened to break up" (Jonah 1:1-4, NIV).*

Prayer

Father,

Thank You for Your grace and mercy! Help me not to return to the very things You have delivered me from and told me not to do. Help me to continue to shun the temptations and the voice of the Enemy that would make me disobey and rebel against what You have done or said. Reveal any areas of my life that are in rebellion and disobedience. Forgive me and help me to return to a position of obedience. I thank You for providing a way of escape when I do come out of rebellion and disobedience because You love and care for me as Your son/daughter.

Amen!

Additional Prayer Points

_____

_____

_____

_____

_____

_____

_____

_____

_____

_____

_____

_____

Reflection

While reading, what stood out to you? What are some things you heard or felt God was saying? What are your key takeaways & how do you plan to apply them to your daily life, or in the future?

_____

_____

_____

_____

_____

_____

_____

_____

_____

_____

_____

_____

_____

_____

_____

_____

_____

_____

_____

_____

_____

_____

_____

_____

_____

Day Seventy-Three

No matter if you are young or old, you have done something you aren't proud of, and you wish you could take back, but don't dwell on that. The Enemy will use your past mistakes to hold you hostage. He will remind you of where you were to prevent you from reaching where you are trying to go. Jesus shed His blood for you on Calvary before you were even conceived, to free you from being a slave to sin and in bondage. He did so to move you into the promises of God as a son/daughter and brother/sister of Christ. The Enemy hates when he can't manipulate your mind with your past. It's when you wallow in unforgiveness to yourself that you remain unconfident in your calling and identity in Christ. So be sure to completely forgive yourself for your past mistakes, whether it was yesterday or 10 years ago because your heavenly Father has already forgiven you.

I challenge you to wake up and tell yourself daily, "I forgive myself because my heavenly Father has forgiven me."

> *"In him we have redemption through his blood, the forgiveness of sins, in accordance with the riches of God's grace" (Ephesians 1:7, NIV).*

Prayer

Father,

Thank You for thinking of me on the cross over 2000 years ago. I thank You that Your grace and mercy cover my wrongs when the Enemy wants to uncover them and leave me naked. Help me to come into agreement with Your forgiveness. I thank You that although I don't deserve it, You made a conscious decision to let me be Your son/daughter and brother/sister through Your blood! Help me to ignore the Enemy who will try to bring up where I used to be to stop me from where I'm going in You. I know You can use my past to help someone else. So help me to change my mindset about the mistakes I've made. Use them to prevent others from making the same poor decision(s) I made.

Amen!

Additional Prayer Points

_____

_____

_____

_____

_____

_____

_____

_____

_____

_____

_____

Reflection

While reading, what stood out to you? What are some things you heard or felt God was saying? What are your key takeaways & how do you plan to apply them to your daily life, or in the future?

_____

_____

_____

_____

_____

_____

_____

_____

_____

_____

_____

_____

_____

_____

_____

_____

_____

_____

_____

_____

_____

_____

_____

_____

_____

_____

Day Seventy-Four

Don't allow the commentary of people around you to stop you from walking in obedience and the confidence God has given you. You will often times feel that when you begin to walk upright with Christ in obedience and moving according to the spirit, not the flesh that you will be criticized more. The Enemy will use that to make you feel you're by yourself and no one is in your corner rooting for you. Whether you know it or not, God has placed people around you who are praying, rooting, and wanting to see you succeed in life and in Christ. People will talk about you whether you are doing right or wrong. Those who were quietly speaking against you in a low season will speak against you louder when they see God elevating you. That is the Enemy's way of deterring you from doing what you have been doing in a low season— being obedient to and confident in God. So, don't get discouraged or step back when people privately or publicly bury your name in the dirt. It may be hard, but learn to grow in it, do right to those who spitefully talk about you, and tear you down. Allow the confidence, patience, and peace of God to flow through you as you continue elevating Him and doing what He has called you to do.

"And those he predestined, he also called; those he called, he also justified; those he justified, he also glorified. What, then, shall we say in response to these things? If God is for us, who can be against us?" (Romans 8:30-31, NIV).

Prayer

Father,

Sometimes I feel that when I am walking in obedience, there are more against me than for me. Thank You for surrounding me with people who are praying for me and truly want me to succeed, but also, You are for me and that's all that matters. I thank You for using how I act toward my enemies as a footstool to elevation, so help me to treat them the same way Christ would treat them. Help me to pray for my enemies and not be spiteful toward them. Help me to understand that You extended Your grace to everyone, including my enemies. Even when the adversary comes and tries to defame me and bury my name in the dirt, help me to not clap back. Speak and operate through me.

Amen!

Additional Prayer Points

_____

_____

_____

_____

_____

_____

_____

_____

_____

_____

_____

Reflection

While reading, what stood out to you? What are some things you heard or felt God was saying? What are your key takeaways & how do you plan to apply them to your daily life, or in the future?

_____

_____

_____

_____

_____

_____

_____

_____

_____

_____

_____

_____

_____

_____

_____

_____

_____

_____

_____

_____

_____

_____

_____

_____

_____

_____

_____

Day Seventy-Five

There may come a time in your life when you feel as though you have done all you can in a certain season. You've persevered through everything that has happened, and there's still no elevation. That is God's way of letting you know there are still things to be learned on that level. The Enemy will come to make you stagnant, complacent, quit, and even try to falsely promote you. It may look like your season will never change, but trust God. He will never promote you prematurely because that can prematurely expose you to things you aren't ready for. God is sovereign, so He knows when you are ready to be promoted. He will test you in every aspect of the next level you are attempting to step into. As the weather outside, seasons are temporary. We may have warm fall weather in December when it's supposed to be winter. We may have cold winter weather in late April, when it's supposed to be moderate spring weather with some rain, but that still doesn't negate the fact that the seasons changed. The delayed change of season, promotion, and elevation do not deny the fact that they are coming. Remember, your season is not a sentence! God always has a specific plan for everything.

So as long as you ignore the Enemy when he comes to make you stagnant and complacent and once you get rid of your timeline and submit to God's, you'll be able to appreciate each season you go through and how long you go through it.

> *"He gives strength to the weary, and to him who has no might He increases power. Even youths grow weary and tired, And vigorous young men stumble badly, But those who wait for the Lord [who expect, look for, and hope in Him] Will gain new strength and renew their power; They will lift up their wings [and rise up close to God] like egles [rising toward the sun]; They will run and not become weary, They will walk and not grow tired"(Isaiah 40:29-31, AMP).*

Prayer

Father,

Help me to wait! Help me to understand that seasons are temporary and will eventually change, no matter how long it takes. Increase my strength when I get weary in my well doing in a certain season, and it feels as if I want to give up. I trust Your plan. I trust Your timing, and I come into agreement with it. Help me not to despise my season of waiting, because You long to bless those who wait. I know waiting produces hope, faith, and expectation. So if I'm waiting longer, my expectation should be growing. I pray against the Enemy that will come and falsely promote me when You specifically have told me otherwise. Help me to know when the Enemy is tempting me to take positions, roles, and opportunities You have not called me to, and I am not ready for.

Amen!

Additional Prayer Points

_____

_____

_____

_____

_____

_____

_____

_____

_____

_____

Reflection

While reading, what stood out to you? What are some things you heard or felt God was saying? What are your key takeaways & how do you plan to apply them to your daily life, or in the future?

_____

_____

_____

_____

_____

_____

_____

_____

_____

_____

_____

_____

_____

_____

_____

_____

_____

_____

_____

_____

_____

_____

_____

_____

_____

_____

_____

_____

Day Seventy-Six

The time comes when you should begin to crave the presence of God in your daily life. You shouldn't just want to feel the presence of God on Sundays or even Wednesdays at Bible study, but you should desire His presence daily. In His presence, there is joy, peace, restoration, deliverance, strategy, and whatever else you need. Sometimes waiting until Sunday and Wednesday just won't cut it because you need it right away. In your day-to-day life, you may have to deal with rude customers or co-workers. Sometimes, there's more month than money or you may have health or home troubles. Whatever the case may be, you should desire God's presence and get into a posture to worship Him. When you turn your worries into worship, God will come and dwell in your praise. If He doesn't come to fix your problem right away, He'll give you the peace you need to persevere until it's fixed. Therefore, the next time you have a frustrating day, you're ready to cuss out the person who cut you off on the road, or the temptation to do something you were delivered from comes back, ask yourself: "Have I been in the presence of God today?"

"You make known to me the path of life; you will fill me with joy in your presence, with eternal pleasures at your right hand" (Psalm 16:11, NIV).

Prayer

Father,

Thank You for this moment of devotion and quiet time with You. Thank You for the opportunity to enter Your presence and hear what You have to say to me. I invite Your presence into my life, Holy Spirit. I thank You that I am receiving the clarity, healing, restoration, deliverance, or whatever else I need from You even now. Create a burning desire for Your presence in my daily life and even now while doing this devotional. I pray that I would have an encounter with You daily to begin to know Your heart and mind, as well as to become more like You. Speak to me like never before. I pray that as I begin to desire and come into Your presence more in my personal life, that I will reach a new realm in prayer, worship, and the things of the Spirit. Help me when the Enemy tries to make me stagnant and prevent me from coming into Your presence.

Amen!

Additional Prayer Points

_____

_____

_____

_____

_____

_____

_____

Reflection

While reading, what stood out to you? What are some things you heard or felt God was saying? What are your key takeaways & how do you plan to apply them to your daily life, or in the future?

_____

_____

_____

_____

_____

_____

_____

_____

_____

_____

_____

_____

_____

_____

_____

_____

_____

_____

_____

_____

_____

_____

_____

_____

_____

_____

Day Seventy-Seven

There may come a time in your life when the Enemy will do everything he can to keep you in bondage, especially when he sees you want out. Desperation is the root of your deliverance and deliverance is necessary action to reach your destiny. Sometimes, God will let you stay in a certain season or situation until you are desperate enough to come out of it. It's one thing to say you want to be delivered, but it's another thing to be desperate for it and do whatever it takes to be free. In the Bible, the woman with the issue of blood was so desperate for her healing that she pressed her way through a crowd of people just to touch the hem of Jesus' garment. Jesus told her that because of her faith, she was healed and delivered from her infirmity. If you stay in certain seasons or situations long enough, eventually, you will become tired of the Enemy holding you in bondage. Your desperation for freedom will bring your deliverance. When your desperation sparks your deliverance, it will make you do anything you can to be delivered. You will never want to go back to the thing or place God delivered you from. God wants the best for His children. He hates seeing us in bondage to the Enemy. So when He sees a heart desperate for deliverance, He meets you right where you are with the freedom you're longing for. In what area of your life are you seeking God for deliverance? Are you desperate enough to break free from the Enemy's bondage?

"And a woman was there who had been subject to bleeding for twelve years, but no one could heal her. She came up behind him and touched the edge of his cloak, and immediately her bleeding stopped. Then he said to her, "Daughter, your faith has healed you. Go in peace"(Luke 8:43-44, 48, NIV).

Prayer

Father,

I pray for deliverance in the aspect of my life that I'm believing You for. Help me to become desperate for deliverance and to do anything I need to do to gain it. I come out of agreement with any demonic force in my body, mind, spirit, and soul. I come into agreement with Your Word that says I am no longer in bondage to sin, sickness, disease, poverty, or anything else that isn't like You! I thank You for the blood that canceled the hold of the Enemy, and I pray that You will manifest that same power and authority over the Enemy. I want to be free from the strongholds that are holding me from reaching my destiny. I know deliverance is a part of reaching my destiny. So I ask You today to deliver me from anything I have knowingly and unknowingly come into agreement with, so I can walk in my full purpose and calling.

Amen!

Additional Prayer Points

_____

_____

_____

_____

_____

_____

_____

_____

_____

Reflection

While reading, what stood out to you? What are some things you heard or felt God was saying? What are your key takeaways & how do you plan to apply them to your daily life, or in the future?

_____

_____

_____

_____

_____

_____

_____

_____

_____

_____

_____

_____

_____

_____

_____

_____

_____

_____

_____

_____

_____

_____

_____

_____

_____

Day Seventy-Eight

You will never learn your significance in life if you keep dwelling on your insignificance to life. God placed you here for a reason, to fulfill your purpose for His plan. Every day is a new opportunity to figure out what your purpose is in life, and if you know what that is, begin to fulfill it. The Enemy loves to manipulate the minds of those who dwell on their insignificance in life. He will make you think you have no reason being here; you serve no purpose in life, and you should just take yourself out, but the Enemy is a liar! God has placed you here on purpose, for a purpose. And every day you wake up is God giving you a new chance to find out what that is. It won't be the easiest thing to find your purpose in life but continue walking with God and focusing on what He has said about you, not the lies of the Enemy. Surround yourself with people who are striving to find or have found their purpose in life. They will encourage you when you hear the Enemy talking. Know that you matter to God. He loves you so much He handpicked you to solve a crisis only you can. Wake up every day and tell yourself, "I am significant because God created me in His image, on purpose for a purpose to ultimately reach my destiny. I will not die until I find it, fulfill it, and bear the fruits thereof!"

"So God created mankind in his own image, in the image of God he created them; male and female he created them. God saw all that he had made, and it was very good. And there was evening, and there was morning—the sixth day" (Genesis 1:27, 31, NIV).

Prayer

Father,

Thank You for creating me in Your image! I thank You that I wasn't created by accident, but You made me on purpose for Your purpose. Help me understand if I get to a point where I feel worthless or insignificant, that I matter and there is a purpose for me on the earth. Help me to understand that every new day is a new opportunity to figure out or fulfill my purpose to reach my destiny. Your will is that I prosper, and I will. So help me to know as long as I am in You, I will win and prosper. I speak against the manipulation of the Enemy that will make me want to give up prematurely or turn against You. Help me to instill the words You have spoken over me that I am fearfully and wonderfully made; I am more than a conqueror; I can do all things through Christ; I am the head and not the tail. I come into agreement with the things You have said about me. I come out of agreement with what hell has spoken over me and the word curses that were sent to break me.

Amen!

Additional Prayer Points

_____

_____

_____

_____

_____

_____

Reflection

While reading, what stood out to you? What are some things you heard or felt God was saying? What are your key takeaways & how do you plan to apply them to your daily life, or in the future?

_____

_____

_____

_____

_____

_____

_____

_____

_____

_____

_____

_____

_____

_____

_____

_____

_____

_____

_____

_____

_____

_____

_____

_____

_____

Day Seventy-Nine

There are no failures in Christ! When you are in Christ Jesus, what looks like a loss is a lesson from Him. Many times, when we are attempting to do something, we are so quick to get it done that we don't consult God for a strategy on how to execute it successfully. Therefore, He will let us lose to learn. Losses set you up for greater success in the long run, so learn to use what you did wrong to change how you do things the next time. Don't allow yourself to wallow in self-pity, sadness, and low self-esteem when you have to learn a lesson through a loss. As my old coach would say, "You can't win em' all, but you can always learn from em' all." So, when the Enemy comes and tries to make you give up after the first attempt, shun his voice and ask God for strategy and direction. If it's something God wants you to do, He will give you the strategy and direction to make it work successfully the next time around.

> *"I am convinced and confident of this very thing, that He who has begun a good work in you will [continue to] perfect and complete it until the day of Christ Jesus [the time of His return]" (Philippians 1:6, AMP).*

Prayer

Father,

Thank You that there is no failure in your kingdom, which means I am not a failure. Even though it may have hurt, I thank You for allowing me to lose to learn. Thank You that losing doesn't make me a failure. Allow me to learn the things You want me to when I experience a loss in my career, business, and personal life. I speak against the Enemy who will try to come in and plant word curses. I come out of agreement with the word curses of the Enemy. I am not a loser; I am not a failure. I will win. I will use what I learned to succeed. Give me the strategy I need to succeed. Help me to seek You for strategies first and follow Your instructions.

Amen!

Additional Prayer Points

_____

_____

_____

_____

_____

_____

_____

_____

_____

_____

_____

_____

Reflection

While reading, what stood out to you? What are some things you heard or felt God was saying? What are your key takeaways & how do you plan to apply them to your daily life, or in the future?

_____

_____

_____

_____

_____

_____

_____

_____

_____

_____

_____

_____

_____

_____

_____

_____

_____

_____

_____

_____

_____

_____

_____

_____

_____

_____

_____

_____

Day Eighty

There's always an opportunity for new chances when you are in God! The Enemy will make you think that just because you failed or lost in a certain area of life, God can't give you the grace to do it again and succeed! He'll even make you scared of something you've never done because everyone around you who failed doing it has convinced you that you will too, but the Devil is a liar! Go back to school! Get that degree! Relaunch that business! If God is for you, failure and fear can't be against you! Many times, the Enemy will use the fear of failure or even the fear of success to hold you hostage, so you don't do what God gave you the grace to do in the first place! Don't live in regret. Don't let the Enemy convince you not to do something God told you to do or try again in the first place!

> *"I can do all things through him who strengthens me."(Philippians 4:13, ESV).*

Prayer

Father,

Thank You for grace and mercy to restore my relationship with you and to try again at the things I may have failed at or taken a loss the first time. I thank You for the chance to take a step back and look at how I can change things and try again. Help me when I fail at something or lose it. Help me not to be bitter, upset, or depressed about it but that I will learn and grow from it. I thank You that even though I lose, I can still succeed. I pray against the Enemy who will make me think just because I failed in one aspect that I'm a failure. I pray against the lies and voice of the Enemy that will try to manipulate me when I am more vulnerable after a loss. I thank You for giving me the strategies even now to try the very thing the Enemy said I could never do again. I thank You that I will not live in regret for not doing the very thing You gave me the grace to do again.

Amen!

Additional Prayer Points

_____

_____

_____

_____

_____

_____

_____

_____

_____

Reflection

While reading, what stood out to you? What are some things you heard or felt God was saying? What are your key takeaways & how do you plan to apply them to your daily life, or in the future?

_____

_____

_____

_____

_____

_____

_____

_____

_____

_____

_____

_____

_____

_____

_____

_____

_____

_____

_____

_____

_____

_____

_____

_____

_____

_____

_____

_____

_____

_____

Day Eighty-One

Sometimes in life, God allows valley or low experiences because He knows they will cause you to turn your attention to Him and enable you to hear Him more clearly. Many times, we despise our bad seasons because we feel a perfect, sovereign and good God shouldn't make us go through them. However, it's in the valleys of life that God's voice is much clearer, and we can gain the perspective we need. It's in your valley that You can seek God's face and get the revelation you need. When God delivers you from your valley, don't allow that to be the only reason you sought Him. Ultimately, your valley experience is used to turn your attention back to God. When you are delivered from it, your attention stays on God. Remember, your valley experience is never meant to break you but bend you more toward God. So the next time you find yourself in a valley, ask yourself, is God using this to turn my attention back on Him?

"When you come looking for me, you'll find me. "Yes, when you get serious about finding me and want it more than anything else, I'll make sure you won't be disappointed." GOD 's Decree. "I'll turn things around for you. I'll bring you back from all the countries into which I drove you"— GOD 's Decree—"bring you home to the place from which I sent you off into exile. You can count on it" (Jeremiah 29:13-14, MSG).

Prayer

Father,

Thank You for my valley experiences. I know they may have hurt me, but they also helped me. Help me learn to focus more on You, to hear what You have to say and take heed to the warnings You give me. I pray that in the valley, I will experience You and Your presence like never before. That after I am delivered from the valley, I can still experience You and grow more in worship and prayer. I pray against the Enemy who will try to make me become stagnant in the valley and miss the things You are trying to reveal to me. Surround me with people who will pray and intercede for my deliverance and breakthrough while in the valley as well.

Amen!

Additional Prayer Points

_____

_____

_____

_____

_____

_____

_____

_____

_____

_____

_____

Reflection

While reading, what stood out to you? What are some things you heard or felt God was saying? What are your key takeaways & how do you plan to apply them to your daily life, or in the future?

_____

_____

_____

_____

_____

_____

_____

_____

_____

_____

_____

_____

_____

_____

_____

_____

_____

_____

_____

_____

_____

_____

_____

_____

_____

_____

_____

_____

Day Eighty-Two

Sometimes, God will send you on a path away from the one you're used to and your state of comfortability because your calling is different and higher. God will take you on a different path that no one in your family had to take, so you will learn to build your faith in Him alone for guidance. It will get discouraging sometimes, and you will want to quit, but that's what the Enemy wants you to do. Yes, it is hard when you know nothing about the places God takes you to get to your purpose and destiny. Yes, it is hard when you know God has told you to do something, and you're the first one to do it, but it is for a reason! God has called *you* to break generational curses off your family line to change the trajectory of your family's future. Don't despise the journey God took you to get to where you are because, in the end, you will prosper and be victorious!

> *"For I know the plans I have for you, declares the Lord, plans for welfare and not for evil, to give you a future and a hope" (Jeremiah 29:11, ESV).*

Prayer

Father,

I thank You that before the beginning of time, You knew me and the plans You had for me. I thank You that when I am in Your will, You will prosper, protect, and give me hope, as well as a future. I thank You that sometimes, the way You take me may get discouraging, but I know You are always with me. Thank You for surrounding me with people I can talk to when I get discouraged or feel alone. I can be vulnerable about how I feel with them. I thank You for using me to break generational curses off of me and my family line. No matter how hard it gets, I say yes to the process. I rebuke the Enemy when he attempts to make me quit. Strengthen me when I want to give in to the Enemy and let me know I will prosper if I continue to hold on.

Amen!

Additional Prayer Points

_____

_____

_____

_____

_____

_____

_____

_____

_____

_____

Reflection

While reading, what stood out to you? What are some things you heard or felt God was saying? What are your key takeaways & how do you plan to apply them to your daily life, or in the future?

_____

_____

_____

_____

_____

_____

_____

_____

_____

_____

_____

_____

_____

_____

_____

_____

_____

_____

_____

_____

_____

_____

_____

_____

_____

Day Eighty-Three

Stop despising God for holding you to a higher standard! No, you can't do what everyone else does around you. He is trying to teach you that where you are and where you are expected to go are much higher. You must learn to act accordingly! Don't allow the Enemy to cause You to act in rebellion because God has separated you from certain people or things. He is preparing you for the people and places He has called you to. If you rebel, you will jeopardize the lives of the people who are waiting for you to get back in alignment with God, so they can be set free! No longer will you be mad at God for setting you apart. No longer will you despise God for holding you to the standard of your calling. God is sovereign, and He is maturing you now, so you won't have to do so when you get to your destination of purpose!

> *"Do not conform yourselves to the standards of this world, but let God transform you inwardly by a complete change of your mind. Then you will be able to know the will of God—what is good and is pleasing to him and is perfect" (Romans 12:2, GNT).*

Prayer

Father,

Forgive me for despising the standard You have called me to live to. I thank You that You are preparing, stripping, and separating me now for the place You want to send me. I thank You that as You separate me from those who will hinder my growth, You will replace them with people striving to be obedient and living at the same high standard You have called them to. Help me to not operate in rebellion but to be obedient to the process. Thank You for setting me apart from others and sanctifying me. I know that sometimes elevation means separation and in some cases, spiritual isolation for a season. I pray against the Enemy who will try to tempt me with the very thing You've told me not to do. I even pray against the people who will try to talk me out of living at the standard You have called me to. Strengthen and give me a way of escape when I want to give in to the temptations of the Enemy.

Amen!

Additional Prayer Points

_____

_____

_____

_____

_____

_____

_____

Reflection

While reading, what stood out to you? What are some things you heard or felt God was saying? What are your key takeaways & how do you plan to apply them to your daily life, or in the future?

_____

_____

_____

_____

_____

_____

_____

_____

_____

_____

_____

_____

_____

_____

_____

_____

_____

_____

_____

_____

_____

_____

_____

_____

_____

Day Eighty-Four

Don't allow the Enemy to keep You in bondage to Your insecurities, past, or qualifications. He wants to do this to keep you away from answering the call of God. In life when you know God has called you, the Enemy will remind You of the insecurities you've overcome, your past you've already dealt with, qualifications you don't need, or even addictions you've conquered to stop you from walking in obedience to the call. The Enemy is afraid of you walking in God's calling and even finding out what His calling is. You may be in a place right now where God has told you to do something or revealed what your calling is but because you have allowed the Enemy's lies to overtake you, you haven't come into agreement with the thing God has said to do. Remember, God won't set you up for failure. You may feel weird stepping out in faith and even feel crazy doing it, but God will complete the work He started in you until He comes back. So don't allow the Enemy to distract you from seeking or answering your purpose in God because His plan is for you to prosper!

"Now the word of the Lord came to me, saying, "Before I formed you in the womb I knew you, and before you were born I consecrated you; I appointed you a prophet to the nations." Then I said, "Ah, Lord God! Behold, I do not know how to speak, for I am only a youth." But the Lord said to me, "Do not say, 'I am only a youth'; for to all to whom I send you, you shall go, and whatever I command you, you shall speak. Do not be afraid of them, for I am with you to deliver you, declares the Lord'" (Jeremiah 1:4-8, ESV).

Prayer

Father,

I thank You for the identity I have in You! Help me not to dwell on my insecurities when You are waiting for me to move in obedience. Help me to understand that You know everything about me, even how many hairs I have on my head. Help me to understand, that if You told me to do it, then I can do it through You who gives me the strength. I pray against the Enemy who will try to tell me that my insecurities are bigger than the anointing inside of me. Help me to shut out the Enemy's voice. I thank You for not setting me up for failure or embarrassment. I pray against the distractions that will even come when trying to seek out my purpose or answering it. I thank You for calling me in the womb. You had a purpose for me when You created me.

Amen!

Additional Prayer Points

_____

_____

_____

_____

_____

_____

_____

_____

Reflection

While reading, what stood out to you? What are some things you heard or felt God was saying? What are your key takeaways & how do you plan to apply them to your daily life, or in the future?

_____

_____

_____

_____

_____

_____

_____

_____

_____

_____

_____

_____

_____

_____

_____

_____

_____

_____

_____

_____

_____

_____

_____

_____

_____

Day Eighty-Five

There will come a time in your life when it will seem nothing is going right. It seems as if it's easier giving up than going through! You may be in a place where the Enemy makes you think God has forsaken you, and you have no reason to keep fighting, but the Devil is a liar! God has not forsaken you. He has you covered. Whether you know it or not, He spoke a prophetic word over you while you were in your mother's womb! He allowed you to be born and still be alive today to fulfill that prophecy. Whatever season you find yourself in, whether it be good or bad, hold on to the word of God spoken over you and let go of the lies of the Enemy! You will get through any season you face. You will survive. You will win and prosper! Don't allow the Enemy to make you quit just before you reach your promise!

"So they got up early in the morning and went out into the Wilderness of Tekoa; and as they went out, Jehoshaphat stood and said, "Hear me, O Judah, and you inhabitants of Jerusalem! Believe and trust in the LORD your God and you will be established (secure). Believe and trust in His prophets and succeed" (2 Chronicles 20:20, AMP).

Prayer

Father,

Thank You for the prophetic word You spoke over me in my mother's womb. I thank You that even when times get rough and the Enemy tries to make me give up and quit on life, I will remember the word You have spoken. You have called me to specific people. I pray as I start walking in purpose or continue to do so You will help me to prepare for those You've called me to. Strengthen me in the times when the process gets so overbearing, and I want to throw in the towel. Help me to realize when I give up on what You've called me to do, I give up on not only You but also the people who I am supposed to bring freedom to. I am very thankful that I worship a man who never lies or has to repent for what He does. So help me to hold onto the words spoken over me by those You've sent to pour into me. Help me to understand that even though I may not see the promise, I still have a promise from You.

Amen!

Additional Prayer Points

_____

_____

_____

_____

_____

_____

_____

_____

Reflection

While reading, what stood out to you? What are some things you heard or felt God was saying? What are your key takeaways & how do you plan to apply them to your daily life, or in the future?

_____

_____

_____

_____

_____

_____

_____

_____

_____

_____

_____

_____

_____

_____

_____

_____

_____

_____

_____

_____

_____

_____

_____

_____

_____

Day Eighty-Six

You may reach a time in your life when you plan, set goals, and want to be at a certain level and in a particular place by a specific age. However, they may not be in alignment with the plan of God for your life. We often feel let down or even depressed in life when we don't graduate in the 4 years society has deemed we should. We feel depressed and unworthy if we aren't married by the age of 25 or have a house by 30. We allow ourselves to get so attached to the goals and plans we have set that we neglect the goals and plans God has set for us. We get out of alignment with the will of God when we forfeit His plan and take ours. Following your plan may temporarily work out but when you reach where you want to be, you will eventually become tired, burnt out, or even not prosperous. Remember to never plan your life outside of the plan and will of God. Trust Him with His plan and future for your life. Besides, when you are in His will, you have no choice but to prosper, be in His safety, and have a hopeful future (Jeremiah 29:11)!

> *"And he who does not take his cross and follow after Me is not worthy of Me. He who finds his life will lose it, and he who loses his life for My sake will find it" (Matthew 10:38-39, NKJV).*

Prayer

Father,

Thank You for the plan You have for me! I come into Your plan and give up the plan I want for me. Help me to understand Your ways are prosperous and although I can prosper by going my own way, it will be temporary. Help me to realize Your ways and thoughts are higher than mine. I understand You may allow certain things to happen that I may not understand until further down the line. Help me not to question so much but to trust You in all things. Help me to always stay obedient and in Your will. I pray against the Enemy that will try to come and make me abort Your plans and do mine. Even when I feel Your plan isn't working, help me to understand You will always lead me to a hopeful future.

Amen!

Additional Prayer Points

_____

_____

_____

_____

_____

_____

_____

_____

_____

_____

_____

Reflection

While reading, what stood out to you? What are some things you heard or felt God was saying? What are your key takeaways & how do you plan to apply them to your daily life, or in the future?

_____

_____

_____

_____

_____

_____

_____

_____

_____

_____

_____

_____

_____

_____

_____

_____

_____

_____

_____

_____

_____

_____

_____

_____

_____

_____

Day Eighty-Seven

Don't allow the distractions of your day-to-day life to prevent you from hearing God's voice throughout the day. Often times, you can get so caught up you forget to hear from God. He doesn't just speak directly to you. Sometimes He speaks through many different facets and channels. The question is, are you alert and taking heed to the voice of God when it doesn't come directly from Him? Be careful how you treat people throughout your day because they could be the very confirmation or answer from God you have been looking for. Never underestimate the ways God will use other people to get what you need from Him. He is very mysterious in His ways and when you put Him in a box, you forfeit the things you need from Him. Allow yourself to open up to any way God wants to speak to you. Shut out distractions and allow the Spirit to speak!

> *"If anyone has ears to hear, let him hear and heed My words." Then He said to them, "Pay attention to what you hear. By your own standard of measurement [that is, to the extent that you study spiritual truth and apply godly wisdom] it will be measured to you [and you will be given even greater ability to respond] —and more will be given to you besides. For whoever has [a teachable heart], to him more [understanding] will be given; and whoever does not have [a yearning for truth], even what he has will be taken away from him'" (Mark 4:23-25, AMP).*

Prayer

Father,

Thank You for allowing me to hear Your voice throughout the day. Forgive me, if I have placed You in a box based on how I think I should hear You. Open my ears to hear You in every facet of my daily life. I rebuke the distractions in my day-to-day life that would hinder me from hearing with clarity the strategy and confirmation I may have been praying for. Help me to realize You can speak through anyone, whether the person consciously knows it or not. Help me to treat others with respect, love, acceptance, etc., as they could be the very channel You choose to speak through. I pray against the Enemy who will try to distract me throughout the day, so I can't hear what You have to say. I pray that if I haven't even heard Your audible voice, I will allow myself quiet time to hear the things You have to say to me. I thank You that I don't worship a deaf or dumb idol. I worship the one, true living God who sees, hears, knows, and answers me!

Amen!

Additional Prayer Points

_____

_____

_____

_____

_____

_____

_____

_____

Reflection

While reading, what stood out to you? What are some things you heard or felt God was saying? What are your key takeaways & how do you plan to apply them to your daily life, or in the future?

_____

_____

_____

_____

_____

_____

_____

_____

_____

_____

_____

_____

_____

_____

_____

_____

_____

_____

_____

_____

_____

_____

_____

_____

_____

Day Eighty-Eight

Life may get hard at times because of the death of a loved one; you're in a low mental state, sick in your body, burnt out on your job or whatever the case may be. Many times, God uses your weakest moments to manifest His strength through you. Whether you know it or not, people are watching you. When you come in contact with people with a smile on your face and a great attitude while going through the hardest times in your life, that's the manifestation of God's strength shining through you. It may be the hardest thing to face your day-to-day life with a smile when all types of things are happening behind closed doors, but how you handle your hard seasons shows God how you can handle your promotion after. You never know who is watching how you handle your hard seasons. Continue to be an example and allow God's strength to manifest through your weakness. Yes, it may be hard to minister. Yes, it may be hard to go to work. Yes, it may be hard to encourage others when you need encouragement yourself. However, God knows if He can trust your attitude in a hard season, He can trust it when He promotes you as well.

"I know how to get along and live humbly [in difficult times], and I also know how to enjoy abundance and live in prosperity. In any and every circumstance I have learned the secret [of facing life], whether well-fed or going hungry, whether having an abundance or being in need. I can do all things [which He has called me to do] through Him who strengthens and empowers me [to fulfill His purpose—I am self-sufficient in Christ's sufficiency; I am ready for anything and equal to anything through Him who infuses me with inner strength and confident peace]" (Philippians 4:12-13, AMP).

Prayer

Father,

Thank You for the strength You give me in my weakest times. I thank You for upholding and strengthening me with Your right hand. I pray that as I go through life, I am able to suffer as Christ suffered. When I feel like giving up, remind me that You have surrounded me with people I can be vulnerable with and talk to about how I am feeling. They will pray and give me the encouragement I need. Help me to realize even in my low moments when it feels as if You have forsaken me that You haven't. Help me to know people are looking up to me, and I am an example of how a person should handle the hard times in life. Yes, it may be hard, and I want to give up, but if I do, that makes the person looking up to me believe it's okay to give up when times get hard. I thank You that even when You suffered on the cross You didn't come down because it hurt, and the people You were trying to help were hurting You. I pray that I will keep the cross in my mind every time I want to give up. May it be a reminder that You didn't give up on me. In the end, I know that how I handle a hard season shows how I'll handle promotion and glory after suffering.

Amen!

Additional Prayer Points

_____

_____

_____

_____

_____

Reflection

While reading, what stood out to you? What are some things you heard or felt God was saying? What are your key takeaways & how do you plan to apply them to your daily life, or in the future?

_____

_____

_____

_____

_____

_____

_____

_____

_____

_____

_____

_____

_____

_____

_____

_____

_____

_____

_____

_____

_____

_____

_____

_____

_____

_____

Day Eighty-Nine

In life, you may get to a point where you have loved, encouraged, prayed, prophesied, and laid hands on everyone else so much that you begin to pour and minister from an empty pitcher. The Enemy will actually try to encourage you to continue to pour from that empty pitcher to burn you out and even make you quit, but don't give in to his manipulating tactics. The Lord loves a humble servant who gives more than He receives, but God also wants you to be poured into as well. Don't allow the Enemy to make you so proud that you don't ask for help, support, and guidance when you become tired, weary, and worn. You need help to continue doing what God has called you to do! Also, be careful of those you are always going the extra mile for who would cross the street for you. Often times, because of your willingness to help, the Enemy will use those people to tire and empty you out as well. Stop tiring yourself out. Understand, you aren't called to everyone. So surround yourself with people who can pour into you just as much as you pour into them. Use spiritual discernment to decipher the Enemy's motives to try to burn you out.

> *"The LORD is my Shepherd [to feed, to guide and to shield me], I shall not want. He lets me lie down in green pastures; He leads me beside the still and quiet waters. He refreshes and restores my soul (life); He leads me in the paths of righteousness for His name's sake" (Psalm 23:1-3, AMP).*

Prayer

Father,

Thank You for using me as Your servant to pour into others whether I know it or not. I pray that as I go through life, I will remember I'm not invincible and that sometimes, I need to be poured into as well. Help me to know that in certain seasons, I should take the time to rest. I need rest to regain the strength to keep being a blessing to others. I pray against the Enemy who will continue to make me want to pour into others even when I'm empty myself. Help me to understand You rested (as seen throughout the Bible), which means I too need rest. Give me spiritual discernment to help me decipher the motives of people the Enemy will use to tire and drain me out. Help me to understand I am not called to everyone. I must surround myself with people who can pour into me just as much as I pour into them.

Amen!

Additional Prayer Points

_____

_____

_____

_____

_____

_____

_____

_____

_____

Reflection

While reading, what stood out to you? What are some things you heard or felt God was saying? What are your key takeaways & how do you plan to apply them to your daily life, or in the future?

_____

_____

_____

_____

_____

_____

_____

_____

_____

_____

_____

_____

_____

_____

_____

_____

_____

_____

_____

_____

_____

_____

_____

_____

_____

_____

Day Ninety

God is saying, "wake up!"

Wake up!

You've been hitting snooze long enough. It's time to take your place!

Wake up!

He has been waiting for you to do the very thing He designed and created you to do!

Wake up!

People are dying daily, but you're still here, which means you still have an assignment!

Wake up!

Prophets, Apostles, Pastors, Teachers, Evangelist, Entrepreneurs, CEOs, COOs, Dreamers, Visionaries, Intercessors, Mentors, Authors, Fathers, Mothers, Sons, Daughters!

Wake up!

Don't allow yourself to leave this earth with your works undone.

Wake up!

"For the creation waits in eager expectation for the children of God to be revealed" (Romans 8:19).

Prayer

Father,

I say yes to Your will!

I say yes to Your way!

I say yes to Your plan!

I say yes to the call, whether I know what it is or not!

I say yes to the process that comes with the call.

I say yes to the good and bad days.

I say yes!

Help me to walk in obedience to the call and purpose for my life. Help me to understand people are waiting for the manifestation, for me to be revealed and walk in obedience to Your will. I pray against the Enemy who will try to make me give up when times get hard, and it feels as though the call is too much for me to carry. Forgive me for despising my call and running the other way or even not answering it because I listened to the lies of the Enemy. I will not hit snooze any longer. I will wake up and get serious about doing the things You have told me to do. I will seek You to find what it is You want me to do. Continue to walk with me daily and help me to understand that Your plan is to prosper me as long as I walk in obedience. Help me to continuously walk in unshakable, unquestionable, and faithful obedience daily and not try to negotiate with You about the thing(s) You have told me to do.

Amen!

Additional Prayer Points

Reflection

While reading, what stood out to you? What are some things you heard or felt God was saying? What are your key takeaways & how do you plan to apply them to your daily life, or in the future?

_____

_____

_____

_____

_____

_____

_____

_____

_____

_____

_____

_____

_____

_____

_____

_____

_____

_____

_____

_____

_____

_____

_____

_____

_____

_____

Conclusion

You've reached the end of this devotional, but don't allow this to be the end of your moments with Abba. I pray that as you go throughout your spiritual journey, you will hold these encouraging words, scriptures, and prayers in your heart. I hope you will revisit this devotional journal from time to time and take another 90-day journey to compare what you journaled the first time with what you hear God saying when you read again. I pray something that was said throughout this book has blessed and encouraged you. I hope it has brought you the healing, deliverance, self-forgiveness, promotion, restoration, or anything else you were believing God for or that it has given you the simple daily encouragement you needed to hear. Encourage a friend to take a moment with Abba to gain the spiritual encouragement, guidance, and clarity he/she needs. I don't take it lightly that you purchased this book. May God bless you and your future endeavors. Always remember: you matter too much to God to give up and quit prematurely!

Made in the USA
Middletown, DE
13 June 2022